The Ranch Table

The RANCH TABLE

ELIZABETH POETT

Recipes from a Year of Harvests, Celebrations, and
Family Dinners on a Historic California Ranch

WITH GEORGIA FREEDMAN

PHOTOGRAPHY BY B.J. GOLNICK

MAGNOLIA
PUBLICATIONS

wm
WILLIAM MORROW
An Imprint of HarperCollins*Publishers*

HarperCollins books may be purchased for
educational, business, or sales promotional use.
For information, please email the Special Markets
Department at SPsales@harpercollins.com.

FIRST EDITION

Designed by Kelsie Monsen
Photography by B.J. Golnick

Library of Congress Cataloging-in-Publication Data
has been applied for.

ISBN 978-0-06-325790-0

23 24 25 26 27 WOR 10 9 8 7 6 5 4 3 2 1

FOR MY FAMILY—

PAST, PRESENT, AND FUTURE

INTRODUCTION

EVERY MORNING, WHEN I LOOK OUT MY KITCHEN WINDOW,
I see the same view my great-grandmother saw when this house was her home. As I warm my hands on a cup of hot tea, I see the sun peek over hills filled with twisted oak trees, big open pastures, and a sprawling orchard. But I also see much more: I see all the hard work and care that my ancestors have put into this land for nearly two hundred years. I see the land where I grew up and where my husband and I now raise our children. And I see the place that I want to protect and nurture and, hopefully, make a little bit better for future generations.

I am a seventh-generation cattle rancher, the seventh generation to live on Rancho San Julian, 14,000 acres of rolling hills, oak forests, and native chaparral on California's Central Coast. This land was granted to my great-great-great-great-grandfather José de la Guerra in 1837 by the Mexican government. My father's family has been working on this land ever since.

I grew up here and spent my childhood helping my parents raise cattle, plant gardens, and care for the ranch. Now my husband, Austin Campbell, and I have taken over much of that day-to-day ranch work, dedicating our lives to building a sustainable system that we hope will preserve and strengthen the land in years to come.

On the ranch, things are constantly moving, growing, and changing with every season. Some parts of our work are predictable: in spring we welcome new calves, lambs, and chicks; in summer we spend long days fixing fences and working in the family vegetable garden; fall brings the final hot days of the year and the last of the garden harvest; and in winter we look forward to rainy days and new, green grasses. But much of what we do is also completely unpredictable. As ranchers, we rely on the land for our livelihood and on the weather for the water and grass we need for our animals. Each season brings surprises, and each year brings both challenges and opportunities.

In response, we change and adapt. Our herd grows and shrinks based on how many animals we can responsibly sustain in any given year, and when we need to, we innovate and come up with new ways to work—and new businesses to try. Over the decades, my family has run cattle, raised sheep for wool, and planted a variety of crops. Today, our main focus is raising high-quality free-range beef in a sustainable way, but we also raise turkeys and other animals; grow lavender to make fragrant oil; sell fruit, vegetables, and honey; and continue to explore new ways to support our family and this land that will bring us into the future.

The one thing we can count on, year in and year out, is that we won't be doing this work alone. Our friends, neighbors, and family members come together over and over throughout the year to help each other out. Whenever there is hard work to be done on the ranch, everyone joins in, providing the extra hands that we could never afford.

In return, we do the same for them. And when the work is done, we all share a meal.

In our community, work and celebration go hand in hand. Food makes our gatherings feel festive and turns a day of hard work into a chance to catch up and enjoy each other's company. I grew up watching my mother feed the crew after brandings and then invite those same friends and neighbors to big lunches and dinners to celebrate holidays, birthdays, and family milestones. These big, joyous events taught me the value of tradition—how marking events and milestones year after year can bring people together and connect us to our past. Now, when I get out the grill to make lunch for a work crew or plan a holiday celebration, I'm carrying on long-standing traditions—and introducing them to my own kids.

For me, this is what food and cooking are all about. Making a meal, inviting people over, and eating together is the best way I know to build community and show appreciation for the people in my life. I also think cooking should be fun! I like to try new things and play with the flavors I love. I'm not a trained chef, and I don't expect perfection from my food. My goal is to make something delicious and to make the people I love feel appreciated. That's what brings me joy. Food is how we celebrate, and it's the time together—whether in a large group or around an intimate table—that really matters.

My biggest hope for this book is that the traditions and recipes that I love will inspire you to build your own traditions and to find the same joy in cooking and eating with loved ones that I do. Use what you find useful here and then add your own favorite flavors and your own twist to things. Keep it simple, keep it fun, and enjoy the moments you have with the people you love in the places you care about.

A SHORT HISTORY
OF THE RANCH

THE STORY OF HOW WE HAVE MANAGED TO HOLD ON TO THIS land and this way of life for so many generations is a story of hard work, ingenuity, family commitment, and lots of luck.

When Rancho San Julian was first granted to José de la Guerra in 1837, it was a parcel of 48,000 acres just inland from Point Conception, the spot on the map where the California coastline curves abruptly to the east and forms the large south-facing arc where the Presidio of Santa Barbara was established. José was born in Cantabria, in northern Spain, and in 1792, at thirteen years old, he was sent to Mexico City to work for his uncle. When he was of age, he joined the Spanish army. He was stationed in California and worked his way up through the ranks before becoming the commandant of the presidio in Santa Barbara. He managed to hold on to the ranch, and others he'd acquired, after California was annexed by the United States in 1850, and when he died, his land was passed down to four of his sons.

José and his wife, María Antonia Juliana Carrillo, had fifteen children who achieved varied levels of success. A number of their sons became politicians or worked in government, and many of their daughters married prominent figures. The most well known of José's children was Pablo Andrés de la Guerra, who represented Santa Barbara at California's Constitutional Convention and went on to serve as acting lieutenant governor as well as a state senator and a judge.

Though José's sons had great ambitions for the family's ranches, they were not particularly successful at running them. After a wildfire, a drought, and financial difficulties, in 1861 they were forced to sell Rancho San Julian, along with other ranches, to their sister, María Antonia de la Guerra, and her husband, Gaspar Oreña. In 1868, the Oreñas sold the San Julian to the Dibblee brothers and W. W. Hollister Partnership. One of the brothers, Thomas Dibblee (who managed the ranches that the partnership had accumulated), married Francesca, Pablo Andrés de la Guerra's daughter—my great-great-grandmother.

The Dibblee-Hollister partnership was prosperous, and together they eventually owned over 125,000 contiguous acres that included the Lompoc Ranch, Point Conception, and Gaviota. In

A cider party on the ranch in the 1980s. That's me, around age two, watching my great-uncle Dibbs work the cider press. The beautiful woman behind me, cutting apples, is my mom.

1874, they subdivided the Lompoc Ranch and established the town of Lompoc. But in 1880, the partnership dissolved, and the ranches were divided. The Dibblees kept Rancho San Julian. In 1910, after the brothers died, their heirs split the San Julian by drawing straws, and Thomas's widow, Francesca de la Guerra, drew the San Julian headquarters—which we call the Casa today—and all the surrounding acreage.

The descendants of the Dibblees and the de la Guerras have worked on the ranch ever since. Francesca's son, T. Wilson Dibblee, managed it until 1952; then my great-uncle, A. Dibblee Poett, took over, followed by my father, Jim Poett, who officially took over in 2000. By the time my father became the manager, the ranch was 14,000 acres; this is the land that Austin and I work today. The ranch is jointly owned by all the descendants of Francesca's children, and everyone continues to maintain a strong relationship with the land and one another.

Above: The de la Guerra family at the first Fiesta in Santa Barbara, in 1924; my grandfather, Harold Poett, is the youngest boy to the left. Right: A barbecue on the ranch in the 1940s.

MY LIFE ON THE RANCH

I WAS RAISED ON RANCHO SAN JULIAN, AND I HAVE SPENT most of my life here. As a kid, I fed cows from the back of my dad's truck, played in the fields with my younger brother, Justin, and climbed trees in my go-to outfit of cowboy boots and a tutu.

I also worked side by side with my parents, helping out in whatever ways I could. My dad taught me ranching skills practically from the time I could walk. He brought me along everywhere he went, and I learned on the go, helping him fix fences, take care of calves, and jumpstart trucks. The summer I turned ten, he gave me a pair of hay hooks and fence pliers for my birthday. He also made sure that I was self-sufficient and understood that if something is broken, you have to fix it—an important lesson for a rancher that has also served me well in every part of my life.

My mom, Marianne Partridge, worked hard on the ranch and at her job as the founding editor of the local newspaper. She also taught me another critical life skill: how to cook. I was very lucky to grow up with a mom who loves to cook and has a relaxed attitude about it. Her kitchen always feels fun. She paints bright colors on the cabinets and invites everyone to come in and sit as she cooks. Her approach is inventive and lively; she rarely follows a recipe, adding "a pinch of this and a pinch of that" to see how new flavors go together or to get a dish just the way she wants it. For her, the most important thing is not just whether her kitchen or her food is perfect—though her meals are always delicious—it's whether the people she's feeding are comfortable and happy.

My mom also never made any rules about what I could do in her kitchen. She let me have the freedom to follow my imagination from a young age; if a dish didn't work out, it wasn't a big deal. She also always let me decorate my own birthday cakes. There were many, many years when that meant it looked like a hodgepodge of different icing colors, but the cake was mine and I was proud of it.

I always felt really lucky to grow up on the ranch, and I've always loved this life, but when I was a teenager, I decided to go out and see more of the world. I went to college in the Midwest, then studied in Spain for a few months and fell in love with the culture and the food. I also spent some time living and working in both New York and Los Angeles. City life was exciting and energizing, but it was not really for me, and after a little while, I felt a strong pull to return to the ranch.

In 2006, I moved back to the ranch full time. As I worked side by side with my dad, I was struck by the magnitude of what he had achieved, not only by building a strong herd but also by using ranching as a tool to preserve the land from development and to strengthen the local ecosystem. Looking at all the care my dad was putting into his herd, I started to wish that we were selling our meat directly to customers, instead of to middlemen, so that people could really appreciate the flavor and health benefits of this humanely raised, grass-fed beef and learn about the connection between the land and the process of raising food and what they put on their plate. So, after a lot of planning, I launched Rancho San Julian Beef, opened a stand at the Santa Barbara Farmers' Market (and eventually another at the famed Santa Monica Farmers' Market), and started selling meat directly to chefs and home cooks. I was so nervous at the beginning, but within a few years, I had developed relationships with home cooks, chefs, and farmers around Southern California, and I learned that I really loved talking to people about where their food comes from and helping customers understand the connection between the land and what they put on their plates.

Shortly after moving back, I met Austin. I first noticed him when he was helping out at one of our brandings. He was a tall and lanky cowboy who looked like a young Gary Cooper, and I immediately wanted an excuse to talk to him. I had spent the day working with cattle and was covered in dirt, but I came up with a reason to start a conversation.

From the very beginning, something felt easy and right about our relationship, and a few years later, we were married before 350 of our closest family and friends. It turns out that between the two of us, we are basically related to everyone in the county, so a big wedding was inevitable. To make it work, we did what our families have always done—we asked everyone to pitch in. We planted a massive vegetable garden and planned the date of the wedding around the harvest. We planted all the flowers for the bouquets and table arrangements, Austin and his friends planted a huge lawn for the reception, and our friends combed through every thrift store for miles to collect plates with mismatched patterns. In the days before the wedding, dozens of people helped cook up a feast. Then we set the tables and threw the most joyous party I could have ever imagined.

And thus began our lives at Rancho San Julian. I continued to grow the beef business and had our two sons, Jack and Hank. Eventually, we moved into my great-grandmother's old home, just up the road from the house I grew up in, where my parents still live today. While my dad still does much of the planning and oversees new ventures and my brother helps with special projects, we have taken on more and more responsibilities, and Austin has become the full-time ranch manager.

Now my days begin when the light pours into the windows of our house and ends when we pull off our boots as the sun goes down. In addition to selling beef, I also raise a small herd of sheep, seasonal heritage turkeys, two pet pigs, and a whole lot of chickens. Taking care of the ranch on behalf of my family, and past and future generations, is an immense privilege and a huge responsibility. Our life here was made possible by the hard work of others, and every decision we make is meant to honor that legacy and carry it into the future.

In recent years I've started a second business, The Ranch Table, hosting classes, dinners, and events on the ranch. We invite people from across the country to come make preserves, bake with seasonal fruit, or just enjoy a meal and a glass of local wine under the wisteria-covered arbor next to the Casa. A couple of years ago, I also took on the unexpected but exciting project of sharing my life and my cooking with people all over the world through Magnolia Network's show *Ranch to Table*. It's been an incredible journey, and for that I am so very thankful.

MY APPROACH TO COOKING AND ENTERTAINING

Whenever I cook or entertain, I remember a word my mom used to say a lot when I was a kid: *tranquilo*. This useful Spanish word means so much more than the English equivalent, *tranquil*. It can also mean "calm," "quiet," "peaceful," "relaxed," and "easy." This is the feeling I always try for when I'm making dinner or getting ready for a party. Instead of rushing around, I remind myself to let go of the idea that things need to be perfect—because that pressure helps no one. Instead, my goal is just to have people together eating good food and feeling at ease. So, I keep it tranquilo and embrace the fun of the occasion. Here are some of the ways that I look at cooking and entertaining that help me keep calm and enjoy the process:

COOKING FOR FRIENDS AND FAMILY IS AN ACT OF LOVE.

I've often heard people say that having people over to dinner makes them nervous, because they're worried about cooking for guests. My response is always the same: *Don't worry so much about the food!* Friends are just excited to be invited over. The point of a dinner party is to enjoy each other's company and do something fun and new. Food is the thing that creates the opportunity to connect, but that doesn't mean it needs to be perfect. Having a meal together should be fun—not only for your guests but also for you. And people always appreciate when you've taken the time to cook something for them, no matter what the food is.

COOKING SHOULDN'T BE INTIMIDATING.

Watching my mom cook meals for family and friends—making dishes out of whatever we had in the house or trying out a new recipe (and always adding her own twists along the way)—taught me that there are no real right or wrong ways to cook. You don't need great knife skills or fancy equipment. If you're new to cooking, start with some basic recipes, but then trust your own instincts. Add ingredients you like and see how things go. If something doesn't look quite right, it might still be delicious. Taste it, think about what it needs, and play with it. You'll learn what you do and don't like in your food, and along the way, you'll get comfortable in the kitchen.

I FOCUS ON WHOLE FOODS, BUT I STILL GO FOR CONVENIENCE WHEN IT'S HELPFUL.

The main ingredients in almost everything I cook come into my kitchen looking like they just came off the farm (even if I got them at the supermarket). I generally like to grate my own cheese, make my own broth, and cut up my own vegetables. This gives me the best flavors, lets me control what my family is eating, and is generally healthier and more affordable! But that doesn't mean I never grab a jar of marinara sauce or a can of beans from the store. I'm a busy, working mom, and getting food on the table can be hard some days. And I think cooking should be fun, not a chore. Similarly, the ranch's gardens are organic, but that doesn't mean I always go to the organic section of the grocery store. Having whole, fresh foods to cook with is the most important thing.

IT DOESN'T TAKE MUCH TO MAKE A MEAL FEEL WELCOMING AND SPECIAL.

When it comes to making guests feel special (or making a family meal feel like the focus of the day), it's the little things that count. Like my mom, I always try to use ceramic plates and simple cloth napkins at my table. But it's not like I go out and buy expensive dishes and silverware. Most of what we use at big events came from thrift stores. If you pick a theme (for example, a dominant color or, say, plates with flowers on them), a mix-and-match set of plates doesn't have to feel like a messy mishmash. I also always put flowers or some kind of natural decoration on the table, even if I'm just going outside and grabbing the flowering herbs from my garden or little branches from nearby trees and vines. Even pine cones and moss the boys pick up on walks can make a nice centerpiece. I also love using old aluminum cans, left over from beans or olives, as vases.

THE COOKING AND PREP SHOULD BE PART OF THE FUN.

When I throw a party, I love doing all the things that happen before my guests show up. I take my time planning, make dishes I enjoy cooking, and get creative when I'm setting the table. I leaf through cookbooks for inspiration and imagine the kind of atmosphere I want to create in my home. I even keep a notebook where I write down the details of my parties, including the guests, dishes I'm planning to make, and other notes to refer back to for inspiration. And if you start to feel overwhelmed by the work . . .

LET PEOPLE HELP!

If you arrive early for a party, I am not shy about putting you to work. I might ask you to pick flowers from the gardens and arrange them on the tables. Other guests help serve at the buffet or carry platters around the table. Our oldest friends come prepared. Some arrange to help with the cooking; others stay late to help with dishes (which gives us some extra time to catch up on each other's lives). We also plan a lot of our parties as potlucks, so everyone can bring a dish they love. Working together makes the "chores" fun and helps us strengthen our friendships and our community.

MY FAVORITE PANTRY ITEMS

Living on the ranch, a good twenty minutes from the nearest supermarket, I keep my pantry and refrigerator pretty well stocked, so that I don't have to worry about running out of ingredients. I use all the same ingredients most cooks always have on hand, but there are a few specific things that I feel really make a difference:

FLOURS

While I always have all-purpose flour for most baking projects, I also keep cake flour and semolina flour in my pantry. Cake flour produces a much nicer, lighter texture in cakes, and it's just as easy to use as all-purpose. (My grandmother was fanatical about using cake flour, and she passed that lesson on to me.) Semolina flour is great for making homemade pasta, which is easier than you'd think and a lot of fun to do with kids.

KOSHER SALT

I always cook with kosher salt. I use Diamond Crystal brand kosher salt in the recipes in this book. It has smaller crystals that dissolve faster than other types. If you use Morton kosher salt instead, be aware that it is about twice as salty (by volume) but takes longer to dissolve, so you'll want to start with half the amount in the recipe, let it incorporate, and then taste your food and add more as necessary. I also have some nice flaky Maldon sea salt to garnish meats, vegetables, and some sweets, like cookies.

SALTED AND UNSALTED BUTTER

Like many cooks, I always use unsalted butter for baking and for cooking things on the stove, but I also like to keep a nice salted butter around just to spread on bread. I really like Kerrygold butter's rich flavor, and I also use it in my flavored butter recipes (like my honey butter and cranberry butter).

GOOD-QUALITY COCOA, CHOCOLATE BARS, AND CHOCOLATE CHIPS

I like to use chocolate with a nice flavor for my baked goods—something I'd want to eat on its own, like Hershey's or Ghirardelli. When I make candy, I always use chocolate chips, not chopped-up bars of chocolate. Chocolate chips have a tiny bit of an emulsifier in them that allows you to melt them into liquid and then cool the chocolate without having to go through the long (and often difficult) process of tempering it.

DRIED BEANS

The Central Coast is a great place to grow beans, and legumes of all kinds are an important part of the local cuisine. Soaking and cooking your own dried beans will give you a better texture and flavor, and it's more cost effective! That said, in pretty much all my recipes, you can use canned beans if it's more convenient.

OLIVE OIL

My go-to oil for cooking is extra virgin olive oil. I usually try to buy California olive oil, to keep things local, and to get something mild that won't add too much of a peppery flavor to my foods.

CANNED TOMATOES, PICKLES, AND JAMS

I do a lot of canning in the summer, not only because it's a great way to preserve produce but also because having high-quality preserved foods on hand makes it easier to throw meals together. I always have whole Roma tomatoes, which I use for pasta sauces, soups, and bean dishes; pickles, which are great as a side for pretty much anything; and, of course, jams, which I put on everything from toast to pancakes and also use as an easy filling in layer cakes.

DRIED HERBS, SPICES, AND CHILES

I often dry herbs from my garden to use later in the year, but I also buy the kind of dried herbs, spices, and chiles you'll find in any regular supermarket. Keep them in airtight jars and they'll last for months. When buying dried chile, you can get specialty chile powders, like ancho or cayenne, but I also keep regular chile powder, often labeled "chili powder," in my pantry. It has a great mild flavor and just a bit of heat.

FREE-RANGE MEAT

I feel very lucky that we are able to raise most of the meat we eat on the ranch. When I do go to the grocery store, I try to support other local producers and get organic or grass-fed meats whenever I can. While many people like to buy their meat fresh, I always have a freezer stocked so that I can have good-quality meat on hand. Once it thaws, it's just as delicious.

TIPS FOR COOKING MEAT

- Always bring your meat to room temperature before cooking it. If you don't, the outside will be overcooked and dry before the center comes to temperature.

- Once you're done cooking the meat, let it sit for a few minutes before you cut into it. (You can put it somewhere warm and tent it with foil if you worry it will get cold.) The residual heat will keep cooking the meat a bit, and all the juices, which get pushed toward the outside of the cut as the meat cooks, will redistribute and settle back into the muscle tissue so that every bite is nice and juicy—and so it doesn't spill out when you cut into it. This is especially important for big cuts, like a tri-tip or a leg of lamb.

- Every piece of meat cooks a little bit differently, depending on many factors, including its fat content and the heat of your oven, stove, or grill. If you want it cooked to a specific level of doneness, it's best to use a meat thermometer.

- The USDA recommends that beef, pork, veal, and lamb be cooked to a minimum temperature of 145°F, which will give you "medium" meat, with a slightly pink center. Ground meat should be cooked to 160°F and will be well done at that temperature. Many cooks, of course, prefer their meat rare or medium rare. I've provided a range of doneness temperatures in my recipes so that you can adjust according to your preferences.

MY FAVORITE KITCHEN TOOLS

My kitchen is well stocked with all the cooking tools you'd expect: mixing bowls, saucepans, baking dishes, measuring spoons and cups, and equipment such as a food processor and mixer. But there are a few tools that I use over and over again, pretty much every day, and also a couple of specialty items that I highly recommend.

A Note on Categorizing Tools: *For me, there is no difference between my grilling tools and indoor cooking tools—most just move in and out of my house depending on what I need. Similarly, I use tools that you might think of as baking tools (like sheet pans) for other kinds of cooking. Just find things that work for you, and use them to make cooking easier!*

FLAT WOODEN SPATULAS

I prefer wooden spatulas with a flat edge rather than traditional rounded wooden spoons, because I can use them to get into the corners of pots, scrape ingredients off the bottoms of pots and pans, and even flip ingredients over as I stir.

TONGS AND SPIDERS

I have a pair of long metal tongs for barbecuing and frying and a shorter pair for cooking in the kitchen. I think of my tongs as an extension of my hand, ready to grab anything hot. I also use spiders, which I call "webs," since that's what they look like—and how they got their name—when frying chicken or making hard-boiled eggs.

CAST-IRON PANS

I collect cast iron like some people may collect shoes. I just love it. I have cast-iron pans in all different sizes, ranging from 8 to 14 inches. Many were handed down from my grandparents, but I have also picked up a few from thrift stores. I prefer them because they hold heat better than pans made of other materials and they're super sturdy—I can throw them on the grill or haul them around in the back of a truck without worrying about them. They just get better over time.

DUTCH OVENS

I use sturdy Dutch ovens for nearly everything that requires a pot, whether it's boiling water for pasta or braising a brisket. If you're going to buy one, I'd get a big one so that it will fit stews, braises, or anything else you might want to cook. A 7¼- or 7½-quart pot is nice and big and will be very useful.

SHEET PANS AND COOLING RACKS

Sheet pans have deep rims on all four sides. This way, you can use them not only for cookies but also for things like making brittle, where it's important that ingredients don't escape over the edge of the pan. I also use cooling racks with a grid pattern that are designed to fit snugly into these sheet pans. They're useful for everything from draining fried chicken to cooling cookies. While you used to have to go to a restaurant supply store to get these, you can now find them pretty much anywhere; they're often called cooling grids.

CAKE PANS

I bake a lot of cakes, but I like to keep them simple, and I don't think you need to have lots of different-size pans. I have two 9-inch-round pans and two 8-inch-round pans, plus an angel food cake pan that I use for almost anything that calls for a Bundt pan—it's just easier to use and to remove the cake from when it's done.

COLANDER AND SIEVE

A sturdy colander is great for everything from straining the solids out of broths to draining pasta and washing lettuce. For dishes that require straining out smaller items—like ingredients in a flavored simple syrup—I use a fine-mesh sieve, which can also double as a sifter.

MORTAR AND PESTLE

I use my mortar and pestle all the time to crush whole spices, mash aromatics like garlic, and make pastes and powders. It offers more control than using a food processor, and the crushing action releases the ingredients' oils and aromas.

CANDY AND DEEP-FRY THERMOMETERS

The key to making caramels or perfect fried chicken is using a thermometer that attaches securely to the side of a pot or pan and can withstand very high temperatures. There are lots of great digital and analog options, but the best ones are sturdy and good for both oil and hot sugar.

MEAT THERMOMETER

The only real way to cook meat to the exact temperature you want it is to use a meat thermometer. There are a few kinds of digital and analog thermometers available on the market. The two I like most are instant-read probes that you can stick into the meat to get an internal reading and the old-school thermometers with a dial that you can leave in the meat as it cooks—though this second type isn't as useful for grilling as it is for roasting in the oven.

DOUBLE BOILER

I have a traditional double boiler—a ceramic insert for a metal pot—that I use for things like melting chocolate and making custard, both of which require the kind of gentle heat you get from steam. You can get the same effect by setting a heatproof bowl over a pot with an inch of boiling water, as long as the water doesn't touch the bottom of the bowl itself; the cooking time may simply be a bit longer.

KITCHEN SCALE

When I first started cooking, I thought kitchen scales were mostly just a waste of precious kitchen space, but boy was I wrong. When I tried one, I realized that having more precise measurements was really helpful. Now I use it all the time. When I measure tomatoes for making sauce, or apples for pie, for instance, it's often a lot easier to just weigh everything together than to cut it up and measure the pieces in measuring cups.

BENCH SCRAPER

These firm metal scrapers are an underappreciated tool. I use mine all the time to scoop chopped ingredients into a bowl or portion bread dough, and especially for cleaning up cutting boards and countertops.

PASTA ROLLER

I make pasta often enough that I really love having a dedicated pasta maker. I use a simple metal one, from the brand Atlas. It's easy to use and it has attachments for cutting sheets of noodles into fettuccine or tagliolini. If you want to try making pasta without a machine, you can also roll out the dough with a rolling pin and cut it into relatively uniform pieces with a chef's knife.

PART ONE

SPRING

BRANDING DAY

MINI BUTTERMILK CINNAMON ROLLS · 9

PISTACHIO BREAKFAST BREAD · 13

ONION-BRAISED BRISKET SLIDERS · 15

with Cabbage and Carrot Slaw 16

SANTA MARIA–STYLE TRI-TIP · 19

PICO DE GALLO · 21

RANCHERS' GARLIC BREAD · 22

TÍO'S BEANS · 25

WEDGE SALAD · 27

with Buttermilk Yogurt Ranch Dressing 27

FUDGY CARAMEL BROWNIES · 29

MINT WHISKEY ARNOLD PALMER · 31

I WAKE IN THE DARK HOURS OF THE MORNING TO THE SOUND of cattle restless in the field below our house. I listen to them shifting about, a sound like leaves rustling, and I hear them call out to each other. It's comforting. It tells me that everything's well, that all the animals are right where they should be.

Today is branding day. Yesterday we gathered a herd of one hundred cows and their calves into the field just twenty yards from my bedroom window. This morning we will move them into the old corrals up the canyon. Brandings are some of the most important events on the ranch every year. They allow us to go through the herd and check all the new calves for the first time to make sure they are healthy—and that they stay healthy. They each get their required vaccinations, and we mark them with our family's brand so that if a fence comes down and some cows end up on a neighbor's property, we can separate our animals from theirs. Our brand is a Y attached to a P; the *Y* is for the Yridises, the part of the San Julian that I live on, and the *P* is for our family name, Poett.

It's four thirty, and my husband, Austin, gets up to start the day. He goes into the kitchen, with our border collie, Gertie, following, and flips on the coffee maker. I hear it begin to bubble away, and the sound gives me the tiny push of energy I need to get out of bed and pull a fleece-lined work coat on over my pajamas. Then Austin is on his way out the door, pulling on his boots and pushing an old straw cowboy hat low on his head. As he climbs into his truck, I hear the cattle guard at the bottom of the hill clang; our neighbors are starting to arrive, ready to help with the work of the day.

I watch the taillights of Austin's truck as it winds its way down the hill, then I get to work too. I heat my blue oven and pop in a tray of cinnamon rolls that have been proofing in the fridge overnight, brew more coffee, and pour it into beat-up thermoses. I have two jobs today: for most of the morning I'll be working in the corrals with the animals, but I'm also in charge of feeding everyone who comes to help, of fueling the day with a steady supply of hearty food and strong coffee. First up, breakfast: to go with the coffee I've made a loaf of pistachio breakfast bread with a layer of sweet, cinnamon-scented nuts in the center, and the cinnamon rolls, which will soon be coming out of the oven, are small enough to eat with one hand. Later in the day we'll give everyone a hearty snack, a sandwich of pulled beef and braised onions with a bit of crunchy slaw. And when all the work is done, everyone will sit down together for a real California-style barbecue feast: tri-tip grilled over red oak, beans stewed with tomatoes and chile powder, thick slices of charred garlic bread, wedges of crisp iceberg lettuce with bacon and homemade ranch dressing, and rich, fudgy brownies with a layer of melted chocolate and caramel in their centers.

By the time the breakfast is ready, my boys, Jack and Hank, are awake and dressed in their Wranglers, button-downs, and boots. Like their father, they dress like ranchers every day—whether they're actually going to be helping out with the cattle or are just heading to school. A heavy jacket and a cowboy hat or baseball cap finish off their outfits. I load the food and coffee into the back of my truck, and we head down to greet our friends and neighbors.

When we arrive, the crew has already started assembling, bundled up in gloves and hats to keep warm: There's Billy King, a cousin, who lives and works on the ranch, and his sister Jenny and her husband, Luke. In my opinion, Luke is one of the best horsemen around (an important skill during branding season). Our closest neighbors are here, including the Mangs, who have lived next to our ranch for more than seventy years. Austin's parents, Greg and Debbie, arrive, and my dear friend Katie Rose Hames and her husband, Will, drive up with their kids. Katie is my oldest friend—we grew up together, playing among hay bales while our parents worked—and Will is one of Austin's friends. Now our own children play together, just as Katie and I did when we were young.

Soon Billy has built a fire to heat the brands, Austin has divided the crew into different working groups, and the branding is in full swing. The crew is a well-oiled machine, and Austin has everything organized to ensure the day goes smoothly. The work of a branding looks the same today as it would have decades or even a century ago. It's the kind of scene you'd see in an old Western—lassos flying through the air, horses thundering by, everyone dressed in well-worn leather chaps and straw hats. If you watch for a while, it's almost like a dance, with riders taking turns and the ground crew running to meet them at the right moment, each person doing their job quickly and fluidly. Some of the neighbors' kids take turns roping, and it's clear they've been learning how to do this for years; the oldest is only fourteen but already holds his own with the adults, roping easily and working ground crew with the skills of someone twice his age. My boys are helping the ground crew with the lighter jobs, learning how the cattle and horses move and how to work as part of the team. It's good to see the next generation of this area's ranchers learning right in front of my eyes.

For much of the morning, I find myself working side by side with my dad, thinking about all the brandings I helped out at as a kid, and the early years of his beef business. My dad officially got into the cattle business on the day after I was born. He and my mom had moved to the ranch with the intention of starting a herd, and seeing his first child must have set something off in him, because the very next day, while my mom and I were still in the hospital, he went off to the local cattle sales yard and bought four steers. As soon as my dad brought them back to the ranch and put them in a field, they circled it, tore through two fences, and headed down Route 1 toward Lompoc.

Thankfully, that inauspicious start didn't turn out to be an indicator of how my dad's life as a rancher would go. In fact, he became a pioneer in the organic meat movement. In 1989, my dad began raising the first organic cattle in California. He sold his beef to local butchers and grocery stores in Santa Barbara County and collaborated with legislators and other farmers to write the California Organic Foods Act of 1990. Over the past decades, he has continued to grow his cattle operation, bringing in high-quality heifers and bulls from all over the country and continually improving the herd's genetics and the quality of the meat we produce.

My dad has always had the utmost respect for his animals and for the land, and his ranching methods are driven not just by a commitment to raising cattle respectfully but also by the idea that good cattle ranching can be beneficial to the environment and help preserve the natural ecosystem, an idea that was radical at the time and is still cutting edge today, though it has slowly become popular with more researchers, academics, and environmentalists over the past few decades. When I started working at the ranch, he reinforced these values in me as he taught me about rotational grazing, the nutritional value of grass, and how to check the herd to make sure all the animals are healthy and thriving.

ψ

As the day warms up, jackets come off and everyone switches jobs. I hand out snacks during breaks, and I hear the occasional pop of a can as people head to nearby coolers for a soda, a Coors Light, or a bottle of water. Around noon, I leave the corrals and start working on the late lunch I'll serve when all the work is done in another couple of hours. The centerpiece of our meal is grilled tri-tip, a classic Central Coast cut of beef that is traditionally grilled over oak. I get a fire started and put a dozen pieces of meat on the grill. My big pot of beans (which I cooked last night) goes next to them to warm up, along with some loaves of garlic bread. My dad comes to help with the grill, and Katie joins us, arranging a platter of iceberg lettuce wedges with ranch dressing, tomatoes, and bacon. She also helps me set out fresh napkins and utensils and arrange cans filled with flowers down the center of long wooden picnic tables.

A branding might be a workday, but I learned from my mom that no matter what the meal, you should always try to make the table feel inviting for your guests. Today, that part is easy; just a couple of hundred yards away is a field of white-and-gold daffodils that a family who lived on the ranch planted generations ago, when we had a dairy building on this part of the property. The dairy is long gone, but the flowers bloom anyway, and it takes Katie and me only a few minutes to pick armfuls of them.

With some good timing and a little bit of luck, the food is ready just as the branding is done and the crew is starting to water their horses and loosen saddles. They carefully put the fire out and clean the corrals, then everyone loads up a plate and finds a seat at the long table. Most of the ranchers pull out their own pocketknives to cut their meat. We eat and joke, and the little valley fills with laughter. We linger for a minute, enjoying the time together, but soon enough, everyone is up and back to work, unsaddling their horses and putting tools onto the back of the trucks. Austin and I load up the dirty dishes, then we, too, head back to the tack room to get everything ready for the next day's work.

MINI BUTTERMILK CINNAMON ROLLS

ACTIVE TIME
30 minutes

TOTAL TIME
5 hours, including rising and cooling

MAKES
24 rolls

FOR THE BUNS

1 cup reduced-fat buttermilk, at room temperature

½ cup (1 stick) plus 2 tablespoons unsalted butter, melted

4 large eggs, at room temperature

4 cups all-purpose flour, plus more for dusting

⅓ cup granulated sugar

1 packet (2¼ teaspoons) instant yeast

1 teaspoon kosher salt

Olive oil, for greasing

¾ cup packed light brown sugar

2 tablespoons ground cinnamon

My small cinnamon rolls are designed for people to eat with one hand (an important consideration for a working day like a branding). They're baked in muffin tins, which helps them maintain their size and shape. After you form the rolls and put them in the muffin tins, you can cover them with plastic wrap and refrigerate them overnight, so that they're ready for an early-morning bake; just make sure to take them out of the refrigerator an hour before they go into the oven so the dough can come up to room temperature.

MAKE THE BUNS

1. Whisk the buttermilk, ½ cup of the melted butter, and eggs together in a medium bowl.

2. Put the flour, sugar, yeast, and salt into the bowl of a stand mixer fitted with the dough hook or a large bowl (if using a hand mixer). Turn the mixer to low and pour the liquid ingredients into the flour mixture. Increase the speed to medium and mix until the dough starts coming away from the sides of the bowl, about 2 minutes. (If the dough doesn't pull away from the sides after a few minutes, add another tablespoon of flour and mix again.)

3. Transfer the dough to a floured surface and knead it until it is soft and elastic, about 5 minutes. Add a little flour as you go if it starts to get sticky.

4. Grease a large bowl with olive oil. Put the dough in the bowl and turn it over a few times so the oil lightly coats its surface. Cover the bowl with plastic wrap and set it in a warm place to rise until it has doubled, about 3 hours.

5. When the dough has risen, turn it out onto a lightly floured surface and gently stretch it out (without ripping it) to form a 12 × 20-inch rectangle. The longer side of the rectangle should be facing you, with the shorter ends on the sides.

continued

FOR THE FROSTING

4 ounces cream cheese, at room temperature

1½ cups powdered sugar, plus more as needed

1 tablespoon whole milk, plus more as needed

SPECIAL TOOLS

Dental floss

Two 12-cup muffin tins

6. Brush the surface of the dough with the remaining 2 tablespoons melted butter. Mix the brown sugar and cinnamon in a small bowl, then sprinkle them onto the dough, covering the dough all the way to the bottom and sides of the rectangle but leaving about 1 inch of uncovered dough along the top (the side farthest from you).

7. Working from the end closest to you, gently roll the dough up into a tight spiral. The edge with no filling (at the top) will stick to the roll; pinch it lightly so that it seals.

8. Grease two 12-cup muffin tins with olive oil.

9. Use a knife to make 24 even marks along the roll (this is easiest if you start with a mark in the center, then mark the halfway point on each side, then the halfway point of those sections, and so on). Use a piece of dental floss to cut each roll from the dough log: scoot the string under one end of the log and cross it over the top, then pull both ends so that the string cuts through the log evenly. Transfer the cut section to one well in the muffin tin, with the spiral up. Repeat, moving down the log, to cut and place all 24 rolls.

10. Cover the tins with plastic wrap and let the rolls rise until doubled in size, 1 to 2 hours (or refrigerate them overnight, then bring them up to room temperature; make sure they've doubled in size before baking).

11. Preheat the oven to 350°F.

12. Bake for 10 to 12 minutes, until the rolls are golden brown. Remove the rolls from the oven and let them cool to room temperature.

MAKE THE FROSTING

1. Beat the cream cheese with a hand mixer in a medium bowl until it's light and fluffy, then beat in the powdered sugar, ½ cup at a time. Add the milk and beat on high until you have a smooth mixture that leaves a thick coat on the back of a spoon but still runs easily; mix in a bit more powdered sugar or milk if necessary to get the right consistency.

2. When the buns have cooled to room temperature, spread the frosting evenly over the tops. Store the buns in an airtight container for 2 to 3 days.

PISTACHIO BREAKFAST BREAD

ACTIVE TIME
20 minutes

TOTAL TIME
2 hours, including cooling

SERVES
8 to 10

Vegetable oil, for greasing

3 cups granulated sugar

½ cup finely chopped pistachios

1 teaspoon ground cinnamon

2 cups all-purpose flour

1 cup pistachio flour

1 tablespoon baking powder

1½ teaspoons kosher salt

1 cup whole milk

½ cup sour cream

½ teaspoon pure vanilla extract

1 cup (2 sticks) unsalted butter, at room temperature

4 egg whites, at room temperature

SPECIAL TOOLS

Angel food cake pan or Bundt pan

This bread was inspired by a friend who once shared his mother's old-fashioned pistachio cake recipe with me. Her version used pistachio Jell-O to give it a green color, but since pistachios are a big crop around here, my version uses pistachio flour (which can be found at some markets and online shops). Many kinds of nuts are grown in this part of California, and I always keep lots of different ones in my pantry to bake with, add to salads, and eat as snacks. This recipe will also work well with other kinds of nuts; try it with almond flour and chopped walnuts or pecans for something a little different.

1. Preheat the oven to 350°F. Grease an angel food cake pan or Bundt pan with oil.

2. Mix ½ cup of the sugar with the pistachios and cinnamon in a small bowl. Mix the all-purpose flour, pistachio flour, baking powder, and salt in a medium bowl. Combine the milk, sour cream, and vanilla in a small bowl; set all bowls aside.

3. Put the butter and the remaining 2½ cups of sugar into the bowl of a stand mixer fitted with the paddle attachment or a large bowl (if using a hand mixer) and beat until light and fluffy; this will take 2 full minutes.

4. In a large bowl, whip the egg whites with a hand mixer on high speed until they hold soft peaks, about 2 minutes; set them aside.

5. Add half the flour mixture to the butter and sugar and beat on low until just combined, then add half the milk mixture and beat until just combined; scrape down the sides of the bowl with a rubber spatula. Repeat with the remaining flour mixture and milk mixture.

6. Add the whipped egg whites to the bowl and, with a wooden spoon, fold them in until they are fully incorporated; you shouldn't see any streaks.

7. Pour half the batter into the prepared cake pan, then sprinkle half the nut crumble over the batter in an even layer. Pour the remaining batter into the pan in an even layer and sprinkle the rest of the nut mixture over the top.

8. Bake the bread for 50 to 60 minutes, until a toothpick inserted into the center comes out clean. Let the bread cool to room temperature in the pan before unmolding and serving. Slice to serve and store the remainder, if any, in an airtight container for 2 to 3 days.

ONION-BRAISED BRISKET SLIDERS

ACTIVE TIME
30 minutes

TOTAL TIME
4 hours

MAKES
*36 sliders, to serve
10 to 12*

One 4½-pound brisket, at room temperature

Kosher salt

Ground black pepper

5 strips of bacon

1 tablespoon extra virgin olive oil

2 large yellow onions, roughly chopped

4 garlic cloves, roughly chopped

1 cup red wine

One 15-ounce can crushed tomatoes

4 cups (1 quart) Bone Broth a.k.a. Beef Stock (page 85) or store-bought, plus more as needed

2 tablespoons granulated sugar

2 bay leaves

36 Hawaiian sweet rolls (3 packages)

Cabbage and Carrot Slaw (recipe follows)

Pulled brisket sliders are a great way to feed a crowd and are also easy to make—after the first few minutes of cooking, you can just put the meat in the oven, walk away, and get other things done. I usually cook the meat and prepare the toppings the day before, then let everything sit in the refrigerator overnight. As the meat sits, it absorbs more of the braising liquid's flavor. Similarly, leaving a slaw in the fridge for a few hours will give the cabbage time to soften and soak up the dressing.

The real key to cooking this cut is to leave all the fat on your brisket (and on any other slow-cooking cuts, like short ribs or chuck). Fat adds the flavor. It will render in the pot and surround the meat, helping it cook gently until everything is tender and delicious.

1. Preheat the oven to 350°F.

2. Cut the brisket into large pieces, roughly 2 inches wide and 6 inches long. Season them generously with salt and pepper. Cut the bacon into 1-inch pieces.

3. Heat the olive oil in a large Dutch oven or heavy-duty pot over high heat, then lightly brown the meat on all sides, 2 to 4 minutes per side. (Don't crowd the pot; cook the meat in two batches if you need to.) Remove the meat from the pot and set it aside.

4. Reduce the heat to medium, add the bacon to the pot, and cook, stirring occasionally, until it's crisp, about 5 minutes. Add the onions and cook for 5 minutes, then add the garlic. Continue to cook, scraping the bottom of the pot occasionally, until the onions are soft and translucent, about 5 more minutes.

5. Add the wine to the pot and bring it to a boil. Add the crushed tomatoes and return the mixture to a boil, then add the broth, sugar, and bay leaves. When the broth comes to a boil, return the meat to the pot, submerging it in the liquid. Taste the mixture and adjust the seasoning as necessary.

continued

6. Cover the pot and transfer it to the oven. Braise the meat until it is tender enough to pull apart with two forks, about 3 hours, checking occasionally to make sure it is still submerged in the liquid. (If the liquid evaporates too quickly, add a little more broth.)

7. Break the meat up by mashing it with a spoon or pulling it apart with two forks.

8. To assemble the sandwiches, split each bun in half and fill it with about 2½ tablespoons of the meat and roughly 1½ tablespoons of the slaw.

CABBAGE AND CARROT SLAW

½ medium head purple cabbage

½ medium head green cabbage

2 large carrots

½ cup flat-leaf parsley, roughly chopped

½ cup seasoned rice vinegar

½ cup extra virgin olive oil

1 tablespoon Worcestershire sauce

¼ teaspoon kosher salt

Ground black pepper

ACTIVE TIME	TOTAL TIME	MAKES
15 minutes	*15 minutes*	*about 3½ cups*

1. Cut out the firm core of each half head of cabbage and discard. Cut each half in half lengthwise, then cut everything crosswise into very thin strips. Toss the cabbage together in a large bowl.

2. Peel the carrots, then use a vegetable peeler to cut the carrots into long strips (not including the light cores). Roughly chop the carrot strips into pieces about 1 inch long. Add them to the bowl.

3. Combine the parsley, vinegar, olive oil, and Worcestershire sauce in a jar and season it with the salt and pepper to taste. Shake the dressing well, adjust the seasoning to your taste, and drizzle it over the cabbage and carrots. Toss the slaw to coat it. Refrigerate for at least 1 hour, or overnight, before using.

SANTA MARIA-STYLE TRI-TIP

ACTIVE TIME
1 hour

TOTAL TIME
1 hour 30 minutes

SERVES
4

One 1¾- to 2-pound tri-tip, at room temperature

3 garlic cloves

2 teaspoons kosher salt

2 teaspoons ground black pepper

⅓ cup soy sauce

⅓ cup extra virgin olive oil

⅓ cup red wine

SPECIAL TOOLS

Plastic spray bottle

Meat thermometer

Tri-tip is the centerpiece of a Central Coast barbecue. The triangular cut, taken from the tip of the sirloin, is flavorful and tender. All you need to do is give it a little seasoning and grill it. (Around here, we use red oak from fallen trees, but any grill will work just fine.) It doesn't even take long to cook. This cut can be hard to find outside California, but if you go to a butcher, they'll be happy to cut it for you.

1. Poke small holes in the fat cap of the tri-tip with the tip of a sharp knife. Cut the garlic into thick slices and put half the slices into the holes, pressing them in so that the garlic fits into the meat without protruding. Flip the tri-tip over and repeat on the other side with the remaining garlic. Mix the salt and pepper together and rub it onto the meat, making sure to use the entire mixture. Let the meat sit and absorb the rub for at least 20 minutes or (preferably) refrigerate it, covered, overnight. Bring it to room temperature before cooking.

2. Heat a wood or charcoal grill to high or a gas grill to medium-high. (If you're working with charcoal or wood, you should have very hot, white coals and only a few final flames; if you're using gas, the temperature should be 350°F and the lid should be closed.) Put the soy sauce, olive oil, and wine into a spray bottle and shake well to combine.

3. Put the tri-tip on the grill fat side down, 12 to 15 inches away from the coals. (Pile the coals to the side of the grill if necessary.) Cook the meat without flipping it, spraying on a little bit of the soy-oil-wine mixture every 5 to 10 minutes, until the fat cap is golden brown, 10 to 15 minutes. Flip the meat, and continue cooking, using the spray, until the tri-tip is about 125°F at the thickest part, 30 to 40 minutes for rare (or your desired doneness); after the meat sits, it will come up a few degrees in temperature and will be medium rare at the center but well done around the edges.

4. Let the meat rest for 10 minutes, then cut it into 1- to 2-inch-thick slices.

VARIATION: OVEN-COOKED TRI-TIP

Preheat the oven to 350°F. Prepare and insert the garlic and rub as in steps 1 and 2 above. Place the seasoned tri-tip in a cast-iron pan and roast it for about 30 minutes (without using the spray), until the temperature in the center of the meat is 125° to 130°F for rare (or your preferred doneness). Remove the roast from the oven and let it sit for 10 minutes before slicing.

PICO DE GALLO

ACTIVE TIME
5 minutes

TOTAL TIME
1 hour 5 minutes

MAKES
4 cups

8 Roma tomatoes

2 poblano chiles

1 medium white onion

½ cup freshly squeezed
lime juice

2 teaspoons kosher salt

½ teaspoon ground cumin

½ cup roughly chopped
cilantro

When I make pico de gallo, I like to cut each ingredient by hand, because I love really tasting each one. If you want a finer salsa to serve with chips, you can follow this recipe but toss it all in a food processor and pulse it until it has a super-smooth texture. The better your ingredients are, the better your salsa will be, so make sure to get the ripest tomatoes you can and always use freshly squeezed lime juice. I use poblano chiles because they have a nice flavor and aren't too spicy for the kids to enjoy. If you want a spicier salsa, leave some of the poblanos' seeds in the mix or swap in jalapeños.

1. Dice the tomatoes into 1-inch pieces. Remove the stems and seeds from the poblanos and finely chop them. Finely chop the onion.

2. Mix the tomatoes, poblanos, and onion in a medium bowl. Add the lime juice, salt, and cumin and mix well. Add the cilantro and mix. Let the salsa sit and mellow for at least 1 hour, so the flavors meld.

3. Store any remaining salsa in an airtight container in the refrigerator for up to 2 days.

RANCHERS' GARLIC BREAD

ACTIVE TIME
15 minutes

TOTAL TIME
30 minutes

SERVES
8 to 10 people

1 loaf soft French bread

2 garlic cloves

½ cup (1 stick) salted butter

When you're hosting a Central Coast barbecue, you always need to serve garlic bread. The buttery slices can be used to turn strips of tri-tip into quick sandwiches or to sop up the flavorful liquid from a scoop of beans. The trick to making it is to scrape the cloves of garlic directly onto the bread; the browned bits of bread will act as a rasp, and you'll get lots of garlic all over. I learned this trick by standing around a lot of barbecues. If you want to make this bread but you're not grilling, you can toast it in a 350°F oven for about 10 minutes, or until it's just getting crispy.

1. Heat a wood or charcoal grill to high or a gas grill to medium-high. (If you're working with charcoal or wood, you should have very hot, white coals and only a few final flames; if you're using gas, the temperature should be 350°F to 400°F.)

2. Cut the bread in half lengthwise and put it on the grill, cut side down, until it is lightly browned, about 5 minutes.

3. Remove the bread from the grill and scrape a clove of garlic onto the cut side of each half loaf.

4. Put the butter in a high-sided, heatproof pan large enough to lay the bread in (such as a high-sided baking pan or an aluminum pan). Put the pan on the grill until the butter has melted. Set the bread into the butter cut side down, press it down, and let it absorb the butter for 1 to 2 minutes.

5. Cut the bread into thick slices to serve.

RECIPE FOR ~~FRIED CHILI~~ *Fried* BEANS

Ingrediants : California pink beans Ⅰ #, 3-4 large brown onions
4 cloves garlic, oregano, marjoram, thyme, season-all,
pepper, salt, Las Palmas chili sauce, petri sherry
½ pound bacon, pork lard, Ⅰ/8 tsp celery seed
Serves about 8

Soak the beans overnight in a large pot with about 3 quarts water;
Boil the beans for two hours or so, tightly covered so too much of
the water does not evaporate. If you have a smoked ham hock, or
bacon rind, boil that along with the beans. Boil until beans are soft
Chop two onions fine, and cut bacon into Ⅰ/2 inch cubes, or smaller
Fry the bacon for about Ⅰ0 minutes until slightly brown, then
add two chopped onions (use a large flat frying pan, preferrably iron)
and Ⅰ tablespoon pork lard. Fry the onions and bacon for about
ten minutes stirring so that neither burns. Before onions turn
brown, add about four large ladles of beans and about two ladles
of their juice to the pan. Mash the beans with a potatoe masher or
wooden spoon. Add Ⅰ/2 cup chili sauce and two or three sprigs of
thyme (I tie the thyme in bundles so that it can later be removed
or one can take the thyme leaves off the stem and leave it in the
beans) (there is no substitute for fresh thyme, but if impossible
to obtain, use Ⅰ/2 teaspoon of powdered thyme). Add Ⅰ/4 tsp. each
of oregano and marjoram and sprinkle liberally with season-all.
Peel and crush 2 cloves of garlic and add. (beans are simmering all
the while) Then add Ⅰ/2 to 3/4 cups of cooking sherry or some other
dry wine . If desired add some powdered garlic, but do not use
too much if it is garlic salt. The fresh garlic is very necessary.
After the beans have simmered for about Ⅰ hour, they should be about
ready to eat, but just before eating, add about Ⅰ/2 pound of
Monterey Jack cheese, if desired- let it melt. If the beans are
allowed to cool and placed in a refrigerator (covered) overnight,
they will be better the next day. I forgot to add the pepper, but
Ⅰ/8 tsp. will suffice any time. You may have to make two frying pans
of these to use the pound of beans. Should serve about 8 people.

Dibb's Beans

Dibb's Beans

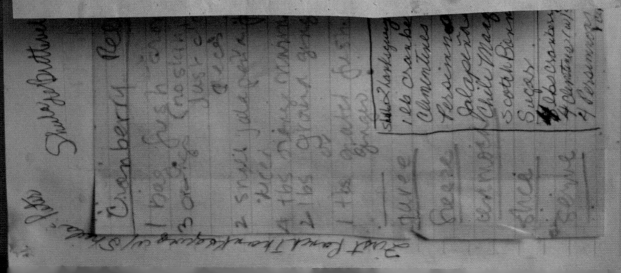

TIO'S BEANS

ACTIVE TIME
20 minutes

TOTAL TIME
3 hours, plus an over-night soak

SERVES
8 to 10

1 pound dried pinquito beans or other small red beans

4 garlic cloves

1 pound bacon

3 small yellow onions, finely chopped

2 fresh oregano sprigs (or ½ teaspoon dried oregano)

2 fresh marjoram sprigs (or ½ teaspoon dried marjoram)

2 fresh thyme sprigs (or ½ teaspoon dried thyme)

½ cup Las Palmas Chile Sauce, Quick Marinara (page 99), or any chile or marinara sauce

⅛ teaspoon celery seed

¼ cup dry sherry

1 teaspoon kosher salt

⅛ teaspoon ground black pepper

½ cup freshly grated Monterey Jack

A big pot of beans is an integral part of a Santa Maria–style barbecue. The most traditional version of this regional bean stew is made with piquintos, small reddish-brown beans that look a bit like the younger siblings of a pinto once they're cooked. They're usually made with a bit of bacon and some ancho and Anaheim chile powder.

My family's favorite bean dish is a little bit different. When we plan a barbecue, we turn to my great-uncle Dibbs's recipe. His version gets extra flavor from dried herbs, a subtle sweet note from a splash of sherry, and a kick from canned chile sauce. (He preferred Las Palmas brand red chile sauce, but any smooth chile or tomato sauce will work.) I still make this dish exactly the way that Dibbs did, following the instructions he once typed out on his old Royal typewriter. Dibbs had a passion for doing things properly. If something wasn't done well, he often said, there was no need to do it at all.

---

1. Soak the beans overnight in a large bowl with about 3 quarts of water.

2. Drain the beans and put them in a large Dutch oven or heavy-duty pot with another 3 quarts of water and 2 of the garlic cloves. Bring the beans to a boil over high heat, then reduce the heat to low, cover the pot, and simmer until tender, about 2 hours. Strain the beans, reserving 4 cups of the cooking liquid.

3. Cut the bacon into ½-inch pieces. Put the bacon into a large cast-iron pan and cook it over medium heat until it releases some of its fat, about 5 minutes. Add the onions and cook them, stirring occasionally, until golden, about 5 minutes. Add the beans and 3 cups of the bean cooking liquid to the pan, stir everything together, and use a wooden spoon to lightly mash some of the beans.

4. Strip the leaves from the sprigs of oregano, marjoram, and thyme and discard the stems. Add the leaves to the pan along with the chile sauce, celery seed, sherry, salt, and pepper. Crush the remaining 2 garlic cloves and add them.

5. Simmer the beans on low heat until the flavors have melded, about 1 hour; if the beans begin to look dry, add a bit of the remaining cooking liquid.

6. Just before serving, stir in the cheese and let it melt.

WEDGE SALAD

ACTIVE TIME
10 minutes

TOTAL TIME
15 minutes

SERVES
4 to 6

4 strips of bacon

1 head iceberg lettuce

¾ to 1 cup Buttermilk Yogurt Ranch Dressing (recipe follows)

2 large tomatoes, cut into 1-inch cubes

Parsley and chives, roughly chopped (optional)

A wedge salad always reminds me of a classic steakhouse. But just because it has an old-school vibe doesn't mean it should be stuck in the past; the combination of crisp iceberg lettuce, crunchy bacon, and creamy dressing is delicious. It's also a perfect side to balance out a heavier meal, like the combination of tri-tip and beans you'll find at a branding. It's easy to prepare, and it's eaten with a steak knife or a pocketknife, if you like to carry your own knife to cut meat, like the ranchers around here do.

1. Cook the bacon in a pan over medium heat until crisp, turning as necessary, about 4 minutes. Break it into small pieces; set it aside.

2. Core the iceberg head and cut it in half, going from the top of the head to the stem end, then cut each half into 2 or 3 wedges, keeping the cuts running from the top of the head to the bottom, so the leaves nestle together.

3. Spoon 2 to 3 tablespoons of the dressing onto each wedge, distributing it evenly. Top each wedge with equal amounts of the tomato and bacon. Top everything with some herbs, if using.

BUTTERMILK YOGURT RANCH DRESSING

4 garlic cloves

1 teaspoon plus 1 tablespoon kosher salt

2 cups buttermilk

1 cup plain Greek yogurt

2 tablespoons freshly squeezed lemon juice

1 tablespoon finely chopped fresh dill

2 tablespoons finely chopped flat-leaf parsley

Ground black pepper

SPECIAL TOOLS

Mortar and pestle

ACTIVE TIME
5 minutes

TOTAL TIME
1 hour 5 minutes

MAKES
about 3 cups

1. Put the garlic and 1 teaspoon of the salt in a mortar and mash them together with a pestle to form a rough paste. (Alternatively, you could use a garlic press and then mix the crushed garlic with the salt.)

2. Scrape the garlic paste into a large (quart-size) jar and add the buttermilk, yogurt, and lemon juice. Seal the jar and shake everything together, then season the dressing with the dill, parsley, and the remaining tablespoon of salt. Add pepper to taste, and shake the mixture well.

3. Let the dressing sit and mellow in the refrigerator for at least 1 hour, preferably overnight.

FUDGY CARAMEL BROWNIES

ACTIVE TIME
15 minutes

TOTAL TIME
3 hours, including cooling time

MAKES
12 brownies

Vegetable oil, for greasing

1 cup (2 sticks) unsalted butter

2 cups granulated sugar

1½ cups unsweetened cocoa powder

¼ teaspoon kosher salt

1 teaspoon pure vanilla extract

4 large eggs

1 cup all-purpose flour

6 ounces semisweet chocolate chips

1½ cups Homemade Caramels (page 253) or 4½ ounces Werther's Original soft caramels, cut in half

2 large pinches of Maldon salt or other flaky sea salt

There is something about brownies that brings me back to my childhood. They are playful, celebratory, and cozy. I like them to be really dense and fudgy, full of rich flavor. This version is a layered brownie with pockets of gooey caramel and melted chocolate in the center. These sugar bombs are perfect for days like brandings, when everyone is working hard and needs a boost of energy—and a fun treat. While I prefer to use homemade caramels for this recipe, I'll often take an easy shortcut and use Werther's Original soft caramels instead; they work really well!

1. Preheat the oven to 350°F. Grease a 9 × 13-inch baking pan with oil and line the bottom and sides with parchment paper.

2. Melt the butter in a double boiler (or a large heatproof bowl set over a pot of simmering water) over medium heat, then add the sugar, cocoa, and salt and stir until the sugar has dissolved and everything is well mixed, about 5 minutes. Remove the top of the double boiler (or the bowl) from the heat.

3. Stir the vanilla into the chocolate mixture, then add the eggs one at a time, stirring until the mixture is silky. Add the flour and stir until it is fully incorporated.

4. Pour about one-third of the batter into the prepared pan; there should be enough to form a thin layer that coats the bottom when you spread it around with a rubber spatula. Bake for 10 minutes, until the batter is barely starting to firm up on top (baking this bottom layer before adding the filling and top layer will ensure that it firms up properly).

5. Remove the pan from the oven. Scatter the chocolate chips evenly over the partially baked batter, then arrange the caramels evenly over them. With a spatula spread the remaining batter over the top and gently smooth it evenly to the edges.

6. Bake the brownies for about 20 more minutes, until the top is just starting to firm up and a toothpick inserted into the center comes out with very moist crumbs attached. Sprinkle the flaky salt on top.

7. Let the brownies cool completely, at least 2 hours, then remove them from the pan and cut into 12 squares.

MINT WHISKEY ARNOLD PALMER

ACTIVE TIME
1 minute

TOTAL TIME
40 minutes, including cooling

MAKES
1 drink, plus extra iced tea

3 unflavored black tea bags

½ cup **Mint Lemonade** (page 113)

1½ ounces whiskey

Ice cubes

1 mint sprig (optional)

Lemon twist (optional)

It probably wouldn't surprise anyone to hear that ranchers enjoy some whiskey from time to time. When we have brandings, I like to offer a slightly different twist by making spiked Arnold Palmers. The drinks are light enough that they work with lunch, and there's something in the mint-whiskey combination that is reminiscent of a classic julep. (You can also customize your drink to give it a stronger lemon-mint flavor by adding more of the base and less ice.) You'll want to make sure you're using an unflavored black tea for this drink, so the flavors don't clash.

MAKE THE TEA

Boil a big kettle of water. Remove the kettle from the heat, add the tea bags, and let the tea sit and steep until it has cooled to room temperature, about 30 minutes.

TO MAKE 1 DRINK

Pour ½ cup of the black tea into a large glass with the mint lemonade and whiskey. Add ice to fill and stir for a few seconds to chill the drink. Poke the mint and/or lemon twist, if using, into the ice on one side of the drink.

BREAKFAST
AFTER A HUNT

BLUEBERRY YOGURT PANCAKES · 37

SAUSAGE AND CHEDDAR FRITTATA · 39

DUCK FAT HOME FRIES · 41

MICHELADA · 43

IT'S A QUIET SUNDAY MORNING, AND AUSTIN IS UP AND OUT long before daylight. In the many years I've known him, I have never seen my husband sleep in. Naturally an early riser, Austin can't stand to waste time. Even his favorite hobbies—fishing and hunting—are hard, physical activities that are really best started first thing in the morning.

There isn't much work planned today, so Austin has gone to meet his dad, Greg, and a friend to hunt some of the wild pigs that live on the ranch. Jack wanted to go, too, so the four of them decided to meet down near the creek while it was still dark out, to try to find the group that we've seen running across the fields in recent days.

Outings like these have been a tradition in Austin's family for generations. Like my family, the Campbells have deep roots in this community; they have lived in Lompoc since Austin's great-great-grandparents moved here in the 1870s. Austin's parents and grandparents all went to the same high school that Austin and his siblings later graduated from, and they know the area as well as anyone.

Austin grew up on ranches just down the road from here, and while his father has a large welding business and his brother became an engineer, Austin always knew that a life on the ranch—the chance to spend every day outdoors, working with animals and taking care of the land—was the only thing that would really make him happy. As a teenager, he took every opportunity he could to work for local ranchers on weekends and school breaks, and as soon as he finished school, he started working for his uncle at the large Cojo Jalama ranch.

Austin's dad and grandfather also started taking him fishing, camping, and hunting when he was young. Those experiences added fuel to his deep love of the outdoors, and these kinds of adventures are still his favorite way to spend any free time he has. These days, he also often takes our boys with him, teaching them the same skills and lessons he learned at their ages.

ψ

Like everything we do on the ranch, Austin's hunting serves a larger purpose. The feral pigs that live in this part of the country are invasive. Most are descendants of pigs the Spanish first brought from Europe and those the US government let loose in the 1950s to kill the rattlesnakes that infested the area where they were building the nearby Vandenberg Air Force Base. These pigs also do a lot of damage to the ecosystem. Unchecked, they'll tear up stream beds and root up hillsides, which destroys native grasses and can cause erosion. They will also ruin crops—one year a handful of the pigs ate all the fruit from an entire field of dry-farmed melons, wiping out months of the farmer's work in just one night. And they'll sometimes go after young calves, too. So keeping the population in check is an important part of our land management plan. And, of course, we eat the meat that Austin brings home, often making it into sausages to freeze for the year.

ψ

When Austin woke Jack around four thirty this morning, Hank (who is still a little young for these kinds of early-morning outings) took the opportunity to stay in bed under a pile of covers. Our house gets really cold in the winter and early spring, so we sleep under a small mountain of flannel and blankets. We also make good use of our three big fireplaces, which are our main way of heating the house. Before going to bed, Austin and I make sure there are low, slow fires going, and in the mornings, the first thing we do when we wake up is add more wood.

Once Hank is up, he and I head down to check on the chickens, sheep, and pigs. Our house sits at the top of a small hill, and the animals are at the bottom, down a short but steep slope. I open up the big gate to the sheep pasture so the dozen ewes can roam around the nearby fields during the day, then we stop at the chicken coop to feed the hens and collect their eggs. Those eggs will be the basis for the big breakfast I'm making this morning. I've decided to make a frittata full of sausage and Cheddar, a pile of sweet blueberry pancakes, and some crispy home-fried potatoes to round out the meal. I'll probably fry up some bacon, too. But to do all of this, I'll need a whole bunch of eggs. Fortunately, the girls have been doing their jobs well, and Hank carries ten back to the house in the front of his shirt. I'll use most of them this morning to make the frittata and pancakes.

Back in the kitchen, I assemble the frittata, filling it with browned sausage, sweet caramelized onions, a heap of sharp Cheddar, and a few chopped tomatoes. While it bakes, I make a huge pan of home fries on the stove. I think about using some bacon fat to flavor them but instead opt to cook the potatoes in duck fat, which gives the dish a rich, decadent flavor. When the potatoes are done, I mix the batter for the blueberry pancakes, which I'll cook right before we eat.

Just as I'm finishing up and making myself a second cup of hot tea, the guys drive up. I make everyone something to drink while I finish breakfast: mugs of cocoa for Jack and Hank and zesty micheladas for the adults. Then I quickly cook up a big stack of pancakes. Austin is in his element, laughing with his father and telling the boys stories about some of their adventures.

Since the day is starting to warm up, we eat outside, in the sun. The food disappears fast—it always does with these guys, no matter how much I make—and soon the boys are having a wrestling match in the grass, and their little dogs, Tommy and Captain, are trying to join in. As they all tumble around, I can't help but laugh; no matter how early we get up, or how much work they do, my kids always have energy to spare.

BLUEBERRY YOGURT PANCAKES

ACTIVE TIME
25 minutes

TOTAL TIME
25 minutes

SERVES
4

1 cup all-purpose flour

2 tablespoons granulated sugar

1 teaspoon baking powder

¼ teaspoon kosher salt

2 large eggs

1 cup whole milk

½ cup plain whole-milk yogurt

¼ teaspoon pure vanilla extract

2 tablespoons unsalted butter, melted, plus more at room temperature for the pan

1 tablespoon freshly squeezed lemon juice

1 cup fresh blueberries, plus more for serving

Pure maple syrup

Pancakes are my favorite breakfast treat to make on a weekend morning. These are on the thinner side—kind of like a cross between a fluffy diner pancake and a crepe—and they have wonderfully crispy edges. I add yogurt to my batter, which gives the pancakes a creamy, smooth texture, and a squeeze of lemon, which brightens up the flavor. When I can get fresh blueberries, I put them straight into the batter, too, then serve more on the side, along with plenty of maple syrup.

1. Mix the flour, sugar, baking powder, and salt together in a small bowl.

2. Crack the eggs into a medium bowl and whisk them lightly, then whisk in the milk, yogurt, vanilla, melted butter, and lemon juice. Add the flour mixture and gently stir until everything is well combined, but don't overmix. Mix in the blueberries.

3. Melt a couple tablespoons of butter in a large skillet over medium heat. When the skillet is very hot (the butter should be almost smoking), ladle some of the batter into the skillet, using roughly ½ cup for each pancake. Cook the pancakes until the bubbles in the batter burst, about 2 minutes, then flip them and cook them for another minute, until they're lightly brown on the bottom.

4. Repeat with more butter and batter until you've used all the mixture. Top with maple syrup and blueberries.

SAUSAGE *and* CHEDDAR FRITTATA

ACTIVE TIME
20 minutes

TOTAL TIME
40 minutes

SERVES
6

12 ounces breakfast sausage, removed from its casing

2 tablespoons extra virgin olive oil

1 medium sweet onion, finely chopped

12 large eggs

1 cup heavy cream

2 cups freshly grated sharp white Cheddar (8 ounces)

1 teaspoon kosher salt

Ground black pepper

½ Roma tomato, cut into ½-inch dice

Chopped flat-leaf parsley

Hot sauce (optional)

My mom is the frittata queen. She makes these filling, eggy casseroles all the time—for family reunions, when she has houseguests, or when people are coming over for a light lunch. They're endlessly versatile and are a perfect way to feed a bunch of people something beautiful with minimal time and effort. I picked up this tradition, and now I make frittatas all the time, too. You can make them with pretty much any ingredients you happen to have around—plus a whole lot of eggs.

1. Preheat the oven to 350°F.

2. Brown the sausage in a large cast-iron pan over high heat until it is well cooked, breaking it up with a wooden spoon as you go so that it has the texture of cooked ground meat, about 5 minutes. Remove the sausage to a plate using a slotted spoon, leaving the fat in the pan; set the sausage aside.

3. Add the olive oil and onion to the pan, reduce the heat to medium, and cook, stirring occasionally, until the onion is very soft and translucent, about 5 minutes; turn off the heat.

4. Whisk the eggs in a large bowl. Whisk in the cream, then mix in the onion, half the cooked sausage, and about three-quarters of the grated Cheddar. Season the mixture with the salt and a little pepper.

5. Pour the egg mixture into the pan. Sprinkle the remaining sausage over the eggs, top them with the rest of the cheese, and sprinkle the tomato in the center. Season everything with a bit more pepper.

6. Cook the frittata over medium heat until you start to see bubbles in the center of the pan and the edges have barely set, about 5 minutes. Transfer the pan to the oven and bake the frittata for 20 to 30 minutes, until it is fully set and golden brown.

7. Let the frittata cool for 10 minutes, or to room temperature. Sprinkle it with parsley and cut it into wedges. Serve with hot sauce, if you like.

DUCK FAT HOME FRIES

ACTIVE TIME
40 minutes

TOTAL TIME
40 minutes

SERVES
6 to 8

4 to 5 medium Yukon Gold potatoes (2½ pounds)

1 cup duck fat, plus more as needed

1 small red bell pepper, finely chopped

1 medium yellow onion, finely chopped

1 teaspoon kosher salt, plus more as needed

1 teaspoon sweet paprika

1 teaspoon garlic powder

These are not your everyday home fries. For this decadent breakfast side, I cook the potatoes in flavorful duck fat until they are incredibly soft on the inside and really crisp on the outside. You can use butter or olive oil instead, but duck fat just takes it to the next level. (It's available in jars in grocery stores.) Make sure to leave the skins on the potatoes; that's the part that will get the crunchiest as it cooks.

1. Halve the potatoes, cut them into ½-inch-thick slices, then cut the slices into quarters, for pieces about 1 inch wide.

2. Melt the fat in a large cast-iron pan over high heat. Add the bell pepper and onion, season with the salt, paprika, and garlic powder, and cook, stirring occasionally, until the pepper starts to soften, about 3 minutes.

3. Add the potatoes to the pan, mix everything well, spread the potatoes into an even layer, and cook undisturbed until the bottom layer of the mixture and the potatoes along the sides of the pan are nicely browned, about 5 minutes. Stir thoroughly, scraping the bottom of the pan with a wooden spoon, then repeat the browning process a few more times, until all the potatoes are fork-tender and many of them are well browned, 20 to 30 minutes total. (If the potatoes start to look too dry as they're cooking, you can add a little more fat.) Adjust the seasoning to taste before serving.

TIP: These potatoes are also great with bacon fat; save it in a jar in the refrigerator anytime you make bacon.

MICHELADA

ACTIVE TIME
2 minutes

TOTAL TIME
2 minutes

MAKES
1 drink

1 teaspoon granulated sugar

1 teaspoon kosher salt

¼ teaspoon chile powder

½ lime

Ice cubes

1 cup **Modelo Especial** or Mexican beer of your choice

½ cup tomato juice

Hot sauce, such as Tabasco

Worcestershire sauce

Lime wedges, celery, crispy bacon, olives, pepperoncini, pickles, and/or cocktail onions

Ground black pepper

Classic micheladas—a combination of beer, tomato juice, and seasonings that originated in Mexico—feel healthier than other breakfast cocktails, thanks to all the vegetables in the glass. (Right?) I particularly like preparing them for guests because it gives me a chance to add all the different kinds of pickles I love to make, like my tart Quick-Pickled Dilly Beans (page 191). Adding lots of garnishes to the glass makes the drinks feel really festive.

1. Pour the sugar, salt, and chile powder onto a small plate and mix them well. Rub the lime half along the rim of a large glass or a pint mason jar, then dip the rim in the spice mixture to coat it.

2. Fill the glass (or jar) halfway with ice. Add the beer and tomato juice, then season the mixture with 4 dashes each of the hot sauce and the Worcestershire and squeeze in the juice from the lime half. Gently stir the drink with a spoon.

3. To serve, garnish the drink with a mix of savory and spicy toppings and some ground pepper.

SPRING CELEBRATION

HOT CROSS BUNS · 51

EXTRA-FLUFFY DEVILED EGGS · 55

ROAST LAMB WITH GARLIC-ROSEMARY RUB · 57

with Mint Sauce 58

ROASTED CARROTS WITH HONEY GLAZE · 61

MOM'S NEW POTATOES WITH BAY LEAVES · 63

VANILLA PANNA COTTA WITH STRAWBERRY SAUCE · 65

CLASSIC LEMON MERINGUE PIE · 67

with All-Butter Pie Crust 70

BUTTER COOKIES WITH FRESH FLOWERS · 71

SPRING ON THE SAN JULIAN IS A BEAUTIFUL TIME. THE HILLS are covered in green grass, and swaths of flowering yellow mustard brighten the sunniest slopes. There are young sweet peas along the sides of the road, thanks to my great-aunt Nanice, who threw handfuls of seeds out her truck window decades ago. All through the fields, native California poppies and lupine offer splashes of orange and blue.

At the Casa—a large ranch-style house that was built in the early 1800s and serves as the ranch headquarters—the flowers planted by past generations of my family are also in bloom. The first roses of the season are opening up on either side of the front gate, and the purple and white irises below the wraparound porch are at their peak. Even the huge hedges of rosemary at the back of the house are covered in delicate flowers.

But the most impressive sight of all is the wisteria. It was planted more than a century ago, and it covers an arbor so big we can seat a hundred people under it. By the middle of spring, the whole structure is dripping with huge clusters of fragrant purple blooms. This is the most magical spot on the ranch at this time of year, and it's where we hold our annual spring celebration.

ψ

Spring has always been an important time for my mom's side of the family. Her mother, Mary Partridge, whom I called Nana, was an Italian American who loved to cook and entertain. She and my grandfather, a racehorse trainer, threw festive parties throughout the year. Easter was an especially big holiday for them. Years later, when I was young, my mom brought her own version of this tradition to the ranch and started hosting a big spring potluck lunch followed by an egg hunt. The party has become one of our favorite family traditions, and these days, relatives on both sides of my family, as well as dozens of neighbors and friends from Santa Barbara, Lompoc, and other parts of the county, make the trek out to the ranch.

Over the years, this party has become a way to bring all our family's and friends' spring traditions together. We organize the meal as a set-menu potluck. The invitation is simple: please bring one of the following items—ham or a leg of lamb, spring vegetables, roast potatoes, a salad, or a dessert. The result is a meal that includes many different people's takes on these dishes but still stays cohesive, so that everyone at the table is eating a version of the same meal. While many guests contribute typical American Easter foods, others bring favorites from other traditions.

To round things out, I also make one item for every part of the meal—a protein, some vegetables, and a potato dish. And I always love to bring a few sweet treats, since I can never decide on just one dessert. This year, I opted to make roast lamb with a garlic-rosemary rub and fresh mint sauce, roasted carrots with honey and thyme, and my mom's classic roast potatoes with bay leaves. I also decided to make some fluffy deviled eggs, hot cross buns for guests to enjoy in the morning, some pretty butter cookies that the kids decorated with fresh flowers, a bright lemon meringue pie, and a batch of delicate vanilla panna cotta with strawberry sauce.

Over the past few years, as my generation of the family has had kids, the work of throwing this enormous get-together has shifted from my mom to me and my cousins Roz Slingenberg and Julie Mott Fabio. They are technically my second cousins, but we grew up playing and celebrating at every holiday and family reunion and sometimes feel more like sisters.

This morning, we all get to the Casa early and set up the space together. By the time our guests arrive, we'll be dressed for a party, but right now it's time to work, so we stash our dresses in one of the bedrooms and stick to old jeans and boots while we haul big bins of plates, forks, cups, and serving spoons out to the arbor. We get a fire started in the enormous, built-in grill so that people will have somewhere to warm their foods if they need to, and I turn on the oven in one of the Casa's three kitchens and put my tray of hot cross buns in to bake.

When my mom arrives, her car is packed with stacks of table runners, more plates and utensils, and armfuls of flowers she has picked from her garden, along with a bunch of golden blooms from the wild mustard in the fields. Our cousin Candida is here from New York to visit her son, Daniel, and his wife and daughters in Santa Barbara, and she comes to help too. The two of them start making the coffee in our enormous percolator and lemonade in a big glass dispenser, then figure out where everything will go—where to set up the buffet, the dessert table, and the bar (a sturdy wooden table and a tub of ice set under some trees)—and how to decorate the tables.

Decorating is an important part of all our celebrations (and family meals) on the ranch, and we always make sure that the tables are ready before guests arrive. We sweep off the long tables and benches under the arbor and lay down the table runners, and Julie starts making dozens of bouquets in old tin cans with her two children, Isabella and Sebastian. We gather armfuls of the lace lichen that hangs from the nearby trees and arrange it into nests that we place down the center of the tables in between the bouquets, then we fill the nests with jellybeans. Last, Roz adds clusters of wisteria for an explosion of color.

Ψ

By late morning, the fog has burned off, and the day is sunny and warm. Guests start to show up, all dressed in their holiday best and carrying their contributions to the meal. Some, like my old classmates from grade school and their parents, have been coming here for so many years that they have a set dish that has become a part of everyone's holiday tradition. For these old friends, bringing their kids to the ranch to celebrate spring is a way of passing on a tradition that they, too, have been a part of for most of their lives. Soon the kids, led by my boys and Roz's two kids, Max and

Madelief, are off on their own, running around the Casa's many yards, climbing trees and playing tag. We let everyone settle in and chat with friends for a while.

At noon, I take Daniel's daughters, Camilla and Linnea, over to the arbor, and together we ring the old dinner bell attached to a post. Everyone gathers in a circle on the lawn, we thank them for coming, and then it's time for lunch. A handful of friends stations themselves behind the buffet (after this many years, the regulars know what needs to be done), and everyone else forms a line for food. Soon the tables under the arbor are full. Friends catch up with people they might not have seen since this time last year and get to know those they haven't met before. One by one, plates empty, and people wander over to the dessert table to help themselves to slices of cake or pie or a few pretty cookies and a cup of coffee.

When the meal is done, we round up the kids and get ready for the egg hunt. Everyone has contributed eggs from their own celebrations, and some of the other parents and I hid them all across the big yards, tucking them behind rocks and flowers in the front area for the littlest kids to find and nestling them high in trees as a challenge for the older participants. To keep things fair, we send the kids out in groups by age, with the youngest starting first, and I'm proud to see that my boys and the other older kids leave all the obvious finds for their younger cousins, siblings, and friends.

For many, the egg hunt feels like a good way to end the day, and the parents with young kids soon corral their little ones to take them home. The remaining guests help themselves to a second cup of coffee and more dessert and sit down in the warm sun with friends for a bit longer. Soon, Roz and Julie and I start winding things down quietly, without disturbing the remaining guests. As people leave, we hand them bouquets from the table, so that they can bring the spirit of celebration to their own homes.

When everyone has left and we've cleaned up from the party, Roz, Julie, and I linger. With our busy lives and young kids, we don't get to see each other as often as we'd like. So on days like today, we take whatever time we can find. We sit together under the arbor, catch up on the news of our lives, and reminisce about past parties. For a few quiet minutes, we can appreciate our time together as a family.

HOT CROSS BUNS

ACTIVE TIME
30 minutes

TOTAL TIME
5 hours, including rising

MAKES
12 buns

¾ cup plus 2 teaspoons whole milk, plus more as needed

3½ teaspoons instant yeast

3 tablespoons warm water (about 110°F)

9 tablespoons unsalted butter, at room temperature, plus more for greasing

¼ cup plus 2 tablespoons granulated sugar

¼ teaspoon kosher salt

4 large eggs

3¾ cups all-purpose flour, plus more for dusting

1¼ cups golden raisins

¾ teaspoon ground cinnamon

½ cup powdered sugar, plus more as needed

My mom has been making hot cross buns every Easter for as long as I can remember, and in recent years, I've developed my own version of this classic. I use golden raisins instead of currants because I like their sweetness and their pretty color—and I use a lot of them to add little pockets of flavor all through the buns. I also like to make each bun big and substantial so that they can serve as a nice breakfast as well as a side. If you want to make these ahead of time, you can prepare the dough the night before. After you shape the buns, you can put the pan in the refrigerator so that the second rise happens overnight. The key is to let the dough come all the way back to room temperature before you bake the buns.

1. Heat ¾ cup of the milk in a small saucepan over medium heat until it is about 110°F. Remove the pot from the heat.

2. Mix the yeast with the warm water in a small bowl, stirring until the yeast has fully dissolved.

3. Cut the butter into large cubes (about 1 inch wide) and put them into the bowl of a stand mixer fitted with the paddle attachment or a large bowl (if using a hand mixer). Add the sugar and salt and beat on medium speed until well combined, about 1 minute. Add the yeast mixture and mix on low.

4. While the mixer is still running, add the warm milk in a slow stream. Turn off the mixer and scrape the sides and bottom of the bowl well with a rubber spatula, then mix on low until everything is well combined, about 1 minute, stopping to scrape the bowl as needed.

5. Whisk 3 of the eggs with a fork in a medium bowl. Add the eggs to the batter and mix on low until well combined, about 30 seconds.

6. Add the flour, 1 cup at a time, mixing between each addition until just combined, about 30 seconds. Add the raisins and cinnamon and mix on low until combined. (As the raisins are mixed in, the dough should start to look a little bit elastic and pull away from the sides of the bowl; it will still be sticky.)

7. Transfer the dough to a floured surface and knead it for 5 minutes, adding a little more flour to the counter if the dough sticks. (As raisins fall out, just stick them back into the dough.)

continued

8. Grease a large bowl with butter. Shape the dough into a ball, transfer it to the bowl, and cover the bowl with plastic wrap. Set the dough aside in a warm spot to rise until it has doubled in size, roughly 2½ to 3 hours.

9. Grease a 9 × 13-inch baking dish with butter.

10. Gently punch the dough down into the bowl, then divide it into 12 equal pieces. Knead each piece on a lightly floured surface for a few seconds, then form all the pieces into balls.

11. Place the balls of dough evenly in the pan, in three rows of 4. Cover the pan with plastic wrap and set the buns in a warm spot to rise until they have doubled in size and are pressing against each other, about 1 hour. (Alternatively, refrigerate the buns overnight to let them rise slowly, then let them come back to room temperature before baking.)

12. Preheat the oven to 375°F.

13. Whisk the remaining egg well in a small bowl. Use a pastry brush to very gently brush the dough balls with the egg wash, being careful not to deflate them.

14. With a very sharp knife, make a ½-inch cut through the top of each bun (you can cut all the way down a line of buns at the same time), then make another ½-inch cut at 90 degrees to the first, so that the top of each bun is marked with an X that runs all the way across the top.

15. Bake the buns for 20 to 30 minutes, until golden brown on top and a toothpick inserted into the thickest part comes out completely clean.

16. Let the buns cool in the pan for at least 10 minutes.

17. Mix the powdered sugar and the remaining 2 teaspoons milk in a small bowl, breaking up any clumps. The mixture should be just thin enough to drizzle but thick enough to hold its shape so that it doesn't spread all over the tops of the buns; mix in a bit more powdered sugar or milk if necessary to get the right thickness. Drizzle a thick line of the frosting down each of the cut lines in the baked buns to make white Xs.

18. Serve the buns warm or at room temperature, directly from the baking dish.

EXTRA-FLUFFY DEVILED EGGS

ACTIVE TIME
10 minutes

TOTAL TIME
30 minutes

MAKES
24 deviled eggs

12 large eggs

½ cup ricotta

3 tablespoons Quick-
Pickled Sweet Relish
(page 192) or store-bought

1 teaspoon kosher salt

½ teaspoon mustard
powder

¼ teaspoon ground black
pepper

1 tablespoon whole milk,
plus more as needed

Smoked paprika

SPECIAL TOOLS

Pastry bag with star tip
(optional)

I like to add my own twist to deviled eggs by swapping out traditional mayonnaise for creamy, fluffy ricotta. It has a milder flavor that lets the eggs themselves really shine, and it gives the flavored yolks a light, fluffy texture. You could also use this same recipe with chopped eggs to make an egg salad sandwich; just adjust the ricotta, relish, and seasonings as necessary to get the same nice, airy texture and a sweet-and-sour pickle flavor.

1. Fill a large pot about halfway with water and bring it to a boil over high heat. Carefully place the eggs into the pot using a spider, cover the pot, and boil for 13 minutes.

2. In the meantime, fill a large bowl with water and ice. When the eggs are done, remove them from the pot with the spider and transfer them to the ice water. Let the eggs chill until cool enough to handle, about 5 minutes.

3. Peel the eggs and carefully cut them in half lengthwise. Scoop the yolks out into a medium bowl.

4. Mash the yolks with a fork, then mix in the ricotta, relish, salt, mustard, and pepper. Drizzle in the milk and mix well; add more milk if necessary to give your yolk mixture a slightly smooth texture.

5. Transfer the mixture to the pastry bag (or a zip-top bag with a corner cut off) and pipe some of the filling into each egg white.

6. Garnish each deviled egg with a light dusting of paprika.

ROAST LAMB *with* GARLIC-ROSEMARY RUB

ACTIVE TIME
10 minutes

TOTAL TIME
2 hours 30 minutes, including the marinating

SERVES
8 to 10

6 large garlic cloves

¼ cup extra virgin olive oil

2 teaspoons fresh rosemary leaves, finely chopped, plus 2 to 3 whole sprigs

1 teaspoon kosher salt

½ teaspoon ground black pepper

One 4-pound leg of lamb (bone-in or boneless), at room temperature

Mint Sauce (recipe follows)

SPECIAL TOOLS

Mortar and pestle

Meat thermometer

A leg of lamb with mint sauce is a classic dish for a spring dinner, especially if you use some rosemary and garlic to bring out the meat's flavor. I make it in a mortar and pestle, but you could use a food processor if you like; the texture will simply be a bit rougher. Just make sure to get it all on the meat; this is not a sprinkle situation!

1. Put the garlic, olive oil, chopped rosemary, salt, and pepper into a large mortar and mash them together with a pestle until the garlic is crushed and everything is fragrant (it will still be pretty coarse).

2. Place the lamb in a large cast-iron pan. Rub half the garlic mixture all over it, covering the meat. Spread the remaining half of the rub on top of the roast evenly so that it forms a ¼-inch-thick layer.

3. Let the roast rest for 1 hour at room temperature or (preferably) refrigerate it overnight.

4. If you've chilled your lamb, take the meat out of the refrigerator and let it sit for at least 1 hour, so that it comes up to room temperature. Top the roast with the sprigs of rosemary. Preheat the oven to 350°F.

5. Roast the lamb for about 1 hour and 20 minutes (to 125°F) for medium rare, 1½ hours (to 140°F) for medium well, or to your desired doneness.

6. Let the lamb sit for at least 20 minutes before cutting into the meat to let the juices redistribute; the meat's temperature will also rise a little as it sits.

7. Cut the lamb into ½-inch-thick slices and serve it with the mint sauce.

MINT SAUCE

1 cup red wine vinegar

1 cup granulated sugar

¼ teaspoon kosher salt

1 cup finely chopped mint leaves

1 tablespoon freshly squeezed lemon juice

ACTIVE TIME	TOTAL TIME	MAKES
10 minutes	*30 minutes*	*1½ cups*

1. Heat the vinegar, sugar, and salt in a small saucepan on low heat, stirring occasionally, until the sugar has dissolved. Simmer to reduce the liquid by about one-third, about 5 minutes.

2. Add the mint to the pot and stir just until it has started to wilt, about 30 seconds. Add the lemon juice and stir again, just to combine the ingredients.

3. Transfer the sauce to a heatproof container and let it cool to room temperature before serving (or refrigerate overnight and bring it back to room temperature before serving).

ROASTED CARROTS
with HONEY GLAZE

ACTIVE TIME
15 minutes

TOTAL TIME
50 minutes

SERVES
6

12 medium-large carrots

½ cup extra virgin olive oil

2 teaspoons finely
chopped thyme leaves

½ teaspoon kosher salt

½ cup honey

When my boys were little, harvesting carrots was one of their favorite things to do in the garden. I would go through with a shovel to loosen the dirt around the row of carrots, and they would dig down and see who was able to get the largest one. It made them laugh and giggle, and it brought me so much joy to see them having so much simple fun.

This recipe is great because it is about as easy as you can get; the carrots and other ingredients are tossed together right on the sheet pan. I enhance the vegetables' natural sweetness with a drizzle of honey—added toward the end of cooking so that it doesn't caramelize too much in the heat—and sprinkle on some thyme, which brings so much fresh flavor.

1. Preheat the oven to 350°F.

2. Trim the tops off the carrots, peel them, and cut them in half lengthwise.

3. Transfer the carrots to a sheet pan and pour the olive oil over them. Sprinkle on the thyme and salt. Use your hands to mix the carrots with the oil and thyme until the carrots are evenly coated.

4. Roast the carrots for about 20 minutes, until tender but not soft (they should still hold their shape without bending when picked up).

5. Drizzle the honey over the hot carrots.

6. Return the pan to the oven and roast for 10 minutes more.

TIP: To make this dish with smaller, thinner carrots, double the number of carrots and leave them whole.

MOM'S NEW POTATOES
with BAY LEAVES

ACTIVE TIME
10 minutes

TOTAL TIME
1 hour

SERVES
6 to 8

25 to 30 new potatoes
or baby golden potatoes
(2 pounds)

½ cup extra virgin olive oil

2 teaspoons kosher salt

½ teaspoon ground black
pepper

25 to 30 small bay leaves
(or 13 to 15 large bay
leaves snapped in half)

Bay laurel trees are native to California, and their leaves have been used to flavor food for centuries. My mom uses them to make simple but incredibly flavorful potatoes. She slides a small bay leaf into the center of each potato, and as the potatoes roast, they absorb all the leaves' wonderful flavor. While the bay leaves are pretty sticking out of the potatoes, you want to remove them before serving—or warn your guests to do so before they eat. You wouldn't want to bite into one!

1. Put the potatoes in a large pot. Add enough water to cover the potatoes by 2 inches and bring it to a boil over high heat. Boil the potatoes for 10 minutes, then drain them.

2. In the meantime, preheat the oven to 350°F.

3. Transfer the potatoes to a tall-sided pan, such as a large cast-iron pan. Add the olive oil, salt, and pepper and mix to coat everything well.

4. Use a sharp knife to make a cut into the side of each potato, as if you were going to cut them in half, but stop two-thirds of the way through so that they don't break open or lose their shape. Slide a small bay leaf (or half a large leaf) into each slit.

5. Roast the potatoes for about 20 minutes, until tender, tossing them once about halfway through cooking. Remove the bay leaves before serving.

VANILLA PANNA COTTA
with STRAWBERRY SAUCE

ACTIVE TIME
40 minutes

TOTAL TIME
*6 hours 40 minutes,
including chilling*

SERVES
6

FOR THE PANNA COTTA

Unsalted butter, for greasing

1½ cups whole milk

One 0.25-ounce packet (2½ teaspoons) unflavored gelatin

2 cups heavy cream

5 tablespoons granulated sugar

1 vanilla bean or
½ teaspoon pure vanilla extract

FOR THE STRAWBERRY SAUCE

1 pound strawberries

1½ cups granulated sugar

SPECIAL TOOLS

Six 6-ounce ramekins

Silky, creamy panna cotta is a super-fun high-impact, low-effort treat. The puddings are stabilized by a bit of gelatin, so you don't have to bake them in a water bath like pots de crème or flan. But the results are gorgeous and delicious—a real wow moment, especially when drizzled with a sauce made from fresh strawberries. They're also a nice dessert for guests who are gluten-free.

MAKE THE PANNA COTTA

1. Grease the ramekins with butter; set them aside.

2. Pour the milk into a small saucepan, add the gelatin, and stir. Let it sit, stirring occasionally (and crushing any clumps against the side of the pot), until the gelatin has softened and disintegrated, about 5 minutes.

3. Add the cream and sugar to the pot and mix well. Cut the vanilla bean in half lengthwise, if using, and use the tip of the knife to scrape the dark interior bits of the bean into the pot, then add the pod as well; alternatively, add the extract.

4. Bring the milk mixture to a boil over medium heat. Stir constantly with a wooden spoon, scraping the sides and bottom of the pot (once it boils, it will come up to the top of the pot fast, so watch out!), then turn off the heat. Let the milk cool for a few minutes, until it is just steaming, not simmering.

5. Stir the mixture well and remove the vanilla pod, if you used it. Pour the mixture into the prepared ramekins, dividing it evenly.

6. Set the ramekins in a 9 × 13-inch baking dish, cover the dish tightly with plastic wrap, and refrigerate until the panna cotta are cold and fully set, at least 6 hours or (preferably) overnight; they should jiggle slightly but be set.

continued

MAKE THE STRAWBERRY SAUCE

1. Reserving 2 or 3 strawberries for garnish, hull and roughly chop the strawberries.

2. Put the cut berries in a medium saucepan with the sugar and cook over medium-high heat, stirring frequently. When the sugar has dissolved, use the side of the spoon to mash the strawberries into smaller pieces.

3. Let the mixture cook, stirring constantly, until it comes to a boil, 6 to 8 minutes. Skim off the foam that accumulates at the top. Cook until the berries have broken down and the mixture has thickened to a jam-like consistency, 5 to 10 more minutes; it will continue to thicken as it cools.

4. Transfer the strawberry mixture to a heatproof container and refrigerate until it is very cold, at least 1 hour.

PLATE THE PUDDINGS

Just before serving, fill a bowl with hot water, dip the bottom ½ inch of each ramekin in the bowl for 10 seconds to help loosen the panna cotta, carefully run a paring knife around the edge of the ramekin, and flip the pudding onto a plate. Spoon some of the strawberry mixture around each one. Cut the remaining strawberries into thin slices and arrange them on the top of the puddings or on the side of each plate.

CLASSIC LEMON MERINGUE PIE

ACTIVE TIME
1 hour

TOTAL TIME
7 hours, including cooling time

MAKES
one 9-inch pie, to serve 6 to 8

FOR THE PIE CRUST

All-purpose flour, for dusting

1 All-Butter Pie Crust (page 70)

FOR THE LEMON FILLING

1¾ cups granulated sugar

6 tablespoons cornstarch

¼ teaspoon kosher salt

½ cup room-temperature water, plus 1½ cups boiling water

½ cup freshly squeezed lemon juice

3 egg yolks

2 tablespoons cold unsalted butter, cut into cubes

I love lemon meringue pie because it's sweet, sour, creamy, and fluffy all at once. Lemon desserts are also my dad's favorite, so I know if I serve one it will always make his day. This is a convenient recipe to make for a party because the crust and filling are prepared ahead of time and chilled; all you need to do the day of is make the meringue and stick the pie in the oven for 10 minutes.

ROLL OUT AND BAKE THE PIE CRUST

1. Preheat the oven to 400°F.

2. On a lightly floured surface, roll the pie crust dough out into a ¼-inch-thick circle that is 16 inches in diameter. Transfer the dough to a 9-inch pie plate and trim the dough to fill the dish and overlap the rim by 1 inch. Turn the edge of the dough under, so that it just reaches the rim of the dish, and use your first finger and thumb to pinch the dough, creating little creases in it, all along the rim. Use a fork to poke a few holes in the dough in the bottom of the pie plate.

3. Line the pie plate with foil, using enough that it overlaps the edges of the dough. Fill the crust with 2 cups of pie weights or dried beans and spread them out so they form a wall against the sides of the crust.

4. Bake the crust for 15 minutes, until the edges have just set. Remove the beans and the foil and bake the crust for another 5 to 10 minutes, until golden brown. Remove the crust from the oven and set it aside to cool to room temperature.

MAKE THE LEMON FILLING

1. Mix the sugar, cornstarch, salt, the ½ cup room-temperature water, and lemon juice in a medium saucepan. Cook the mixture on low, stirring until everything has just combined. Add the egg yolks, one at a time, stirring constantly. Add the butter and stir until it has melted. Add the 1½ cups boiling water while stirring constantly.

2. Simmer the mixture, continuing to stir constantly, until it has the texture of a thick pudding (which will happen quickly). Immediately remove it from the heat and pour it into the prepared crust; smooth the top with a rubber spatula.

3. Refrigerate the pie for at least 6 hours or (preferably) overnight.

continued

FOR THE MERINGUE

9 egg whites

1½ teaspoons pure vanilla extract

¾ cup granulated sugar

½ teaspoon cream of tartar

SPECIAL TOOLS

Pie weights (or dried beans)

Pastry bag with a star tip (optional)

MAKE THE MERINGUE

1. Preheat the oven to 350°F.

2. Use a hand mixer to beat the egg whites on high speed until very frothy. Add the vanilla and mix on high speed until it is incorporated. Add the sugar and cream of tartar, then continue beating the mixture on high until the egg whites hold a stiff peak.

3. Spoon two-thirds of the meringue evenly onto the chilled pie, covering the lemon filling, then use a rubber spatula to smooth the meringue, starting at the crust and working your way from the outside of the pie to the center to shape it into a dome. Put the remaining meringue in a pastry bag with a star tip (if using) and use it to decorate the top of the pie: With a gentle squeezing motion, make a ring of ½-inch-tall meringue stars all around the edge, next to the crust. Make another ring of stars just inside the first, then continue making smaller and smaller rings of stars, one inside the other, until you've covered the entire dome. Alternatively, use a butter knife to spread the remaining meringue onto the top of the pie in decorative swirls.

4. Bake the pie for 5 to 10 minutes, until the tips of the meringue are golden brown. Let the pie cool for 10 minutes before serving.

ALL-BUTTER PIE CRUST

ACTIVE TIME
10 minutes

TOTAL TIME
*2 hours 10 minutes,
including chilling*

MAKES
*1 crust (for a
single-crust pie)*

1½ cups all-purpose flour,
plus more for dusting

½ cup (1 stick) cold
unsalted butter, cut into
small cubes

2 tablespoons granulated
sugar

½ teaspoon kosher salt

¼ cup ice-cold water

This classic, versatile crust can be used for pretty much any kind of pie, from lemon meringue (page 67) to apple (page 221). It's easy to make and comes together quickly, but it still has the light, flaky quality you want in a crust. I make it in the food processor, rather than cutting the butter into the flour with a fork or rubbing it with my fingers, because it's faster and easier and keeps the butter cold, which is what brings in all that flakiness. I often make it ahead of time if I know I'm going to make pie later in the week, and sometimes I'll even throw a disk into the freezer for the future; it's as convenient as buying one premade but has much better flavor.

This recipe makes enough crust for a pie with just a bottom crust. For a double-crust pie (like my apple pie, which uses the ginger variation below), double the recipe and divide the dough into two even disks before refrigerating it.

1. Put the flour, butter, sugar, and salt in a food processor. Pulse until the mixture looks gritty. Continue to pulse as you slowly add the ice water. Stop pulsing when the mixture holds together in a ball when you squeeze it.

2. Turn the dough out onto a floured surface and press it into a flattened disk. Wrap it in plastic wrap and refrigerate it for at least 2 hours.

VARIATION: GINGER PIE CRUST

To make a ginger-flavored pie crust for my Spiced Honey Apple Pie (page 221), double the recipe above (so you have enough dough for both a top and bottom crust), add 2 teaspoons ground ginger and 1 teaspoon finely grated fresh ginger with the flour, butter, sugar, and salt, and divide the dough into two disks before chilling it. (I freeze my ginger before grating it to make it easier to work with.)

BUTTER COOKIES *with* FRESH FLOWERS

ACTIVE TIME
25 minutes

TOTAL TIME
4 hours, including chilling

MAKES
20 cookies

1 cup (2 sticks) unsalted butter, at room temperature, cut into cubes

½ cup granulated sugar

1 large egg, separated

1 teaspoon pure vanilla extract

2 cups all-purpose flour, plus more for rolling out the dough

½ teaspoon kosher salt

Edible flowers, such as rose petals, lavender, sage blossoms, thyme blossoms, marigolds, or violets

Turbinado sugar

These beautiful treats were inspired by the flavor of Danish butter cookies. We sometimes find this kind of cookie in Solvang, a town about twenty miles from the ranch that was founded by Danish settlers in 1911. It's now a popular tourist spot—and home to some really great food! Mine is a simpler version of this classic treat: I roll the dough into a long cylinder, refrigerate it, slice it into rounds, and decorate each slice with edible flowers. I usually use things from my garden, such as rose petals or blossoms from my herbs, including rosemary, lavender, and thyme. It's a fun project to do with kids before a big party, and the result is really beautiful. You can also make the dough ahead of time and freeze it, and then let it thaw in the refrigerator before slicing.

---

1. Put the butter and sugar into the bowl of a stand mixer fitted with the paddle attachment or a large bowl (if using a hand mixer) and beat them together on medium speed until the mixture is light and fluffy, about 3 minutes. Scrape the bowl with a rubber spatula and beat the mixture for a few more seconds until well combined.

2. Add the egg yolk and vanilla to the mixer and beat on medium until well combined, about 1 minute.

3. Add 1 cup of the flour and the salt and beat on low until just combined, about 30 seconds. Add the remaining 1 cup flour and beat for 1 minute, scraping the bowl a couple of times to make sure everything is incorporated.

4. Turn the dough out onto a lightly floured surface and roll it into a log 10 inches long and 2 inches in diameter, making sure it has a nice round shape and is evenly thick from one end to the other (this will determine the shape and size of your cookies). Wrap the log with two layers of plastic wrap and chill it for a minimum of 3 hours, or (preferably) overnight, to make sure it is very cold all the way through. (Refrigerate the egg white as well.)

5. Preheat the oven to 350°F. Line two sheet pans with parchment paper.

6. Unwrap the log of dough and cut it in half crosswise. (If you see that the center isn't totally firm at this point, refrigerate it longer.) Rewrap half of the log and return it to the refrigerator while you prepare the first batch.

continued

7. Mark the remaining half log with 9 evenly spaced lines (they should be ½ inch apart), then use a very sharp knife to cut the log at those points so you have 10 even circles.

8. Lay the rounds on one of the prepared sheet pans, spacing them evenly. (If there are air holes in the dough, use your finger to gently press the dough together at those spots.)

9. Press a flower (or a couple of large flower petals) onto the top of each round, pushing hard enough to stick the flower firmly to the dough but not so hard that you change the cookie's shape.

10. Whisk the egg white in a small bowl until it is loose and fluid and brush some gently on the top of each cookie. Sprinkle a good pinch of turbinado sugar over each cookie.

11. Bake the cookies for 12 to 15 minutes, until golden all over. (While the first batch of cookies is in the oven, prepare the second batch, starting from step 7.) Remove the sheet pan from the oven and bake the second batch. Let each batch of cookies cool for 5 minutes on the pan, then gently move them to a rack to cool to room temperature before serving. Store the cookies in an airtight container for 2 to 3 days.

PART TWO

SUMMER

Tailgate After a Gather

Birthday Dinner in the Lavender Field

Fiesta Family Reunion

Beach Cookout

TAILGATE AFTER
A GATHER

LAYERED AVOCADO DIP · 81

RANCHERS' BEEF CHILI · 83
with Bone Broth a.k.a. Beef Stock 85

CAST-IRON CORN BREAD · 87
with Honey Butter 87

IF YOU ASK SOMEONE TO PICTURE WHAT CATTLE RANCHING might look like, chances are the image will be a scene of cowboys pushing a herd of cows across the countryside. This might seem like something out of an old Western, but the reality is, gathering cattle on horseback is still an important part of ranch life, especially on a ranch like the San Julian. While other places, like Texas, have big, flat prairies that are accessible by truck or ATV, the Central Coast is full of rocky hills and dense oak forest. The only way to get to many spots is to ride or walk. So when it's time to gather the herd, we are almost always on horseback.

I've been riding horses for as long as I can remember. When I was really little, my dad would often hold me in front of him as he rode. These days, I usually ride Niño. He is a sweet horse, but he acts like a little kid. He has tons of energy, and at the beginning of every ride he gets distracted by everything and acts like he's never seen a tree before—even though he's been working in these same hills for years. He's a ridiculous character, but at this point we know each other well enough, and I know what to expect.

Today, Niño is as excited as usual and nods his head up and down when I bring him into the horse barn. It's time to move some cattle, so Austin, Billy King, and some friends and I are going to spend the late afternoon gathering one of the herds and moving them into the next pasture. Niño knows the drill, and he's excited for the ride—and for the hay he'll have when we get back.

We meet at the tack room, where we keep all our saddles, blankets, and gear. The room sits a few steps up in the horse barn and has a warm, reddish wood floor and dusty whitewashed walls. It's also decorated with old family photographs of the stagecoaches that used to pass by this very barn on the way from Santa Barbara to Lompoc a century ago.

I love the smell of this place, a combination of alfalfa, old leather, and horse sweat drying under the saddle blankets. Two windows with ancient wavy glass panes let in a beautiful kind of golden light that hits every single dust particle hanging in the air and makes the room feel almost magical. The walls are lined with reins and chaps on hooks made of old horseshoes. Over the years, the tack room and barn have almost become a bit of a hangout area, with a fridge stocked with beer (for the adults) and juice (for the kids). Like many spots on the ranch, this building is an important part of our work but also a place where we can relax and hang out after a long day.

I brush and saddle Niño, and we load up in the horse trailer and drive the four miles to the Yridises, the part of the ranch that I live on. It's best to move cattle when the weather is cool and comfortable, so we've waited until this time of day to begin, and I can already feel the early-summer heat lifting. We unload our horses and head out, along with our border collie, Gertie, and Billy's dog, Penny.

Ψ

Moving cattle from one pasture to another throughout the year is a process known as rotational grazing, and it is an important part of the work we do on the San Julian. It's how we ensure that the land will be healthy and fertile for generations to come. The timing for moving cattle depends on everything from the size of the herd to the size of the pasture to how much rain we had earlier in the year. About half the work we do on the ranch is what we call "checking cows," which means not just checking to see that the animals are healthy and that the spring boxes and water troughs are working but also how the grasses in the pastures are holding up. When the grass starts to look short, we move the cows off it, so that it will be strong enough to regrow and reseed itself for the following year. The manure that the cows have worked into the land as they go also provides the grass with a natural fertilizer.

ψ

We line out across the top of a hillside and move forward, and the cows and their calves start to move away in front of us, down the canyon and toward the lower part of the ranch. Things go smoothly today, with no surprises or stubborn animals, so after a couple of hours, once we've crossed most of the pasture, I decide to head back to the house to get the meal that I had prepared earlier in the day for the crew. On afternoons like these, everyone wants to eat quickly and then head back to their homes, so to make things easy I will bring the food to them. I've made a big pot of chili that I warm up in the oven, and once I wrap it in some kitchen towels, I can wedge it onto the floor of my truck and I'm good to go. I also have a big container of layered dip waiting in the refrigerator. A skillet of corn bread that's been resting on my stove will be served with big dollops of honey butter to round out the meal.

By the time I'm back, the riders are on their way to the trucks and trailers. I park the rusted 1962 Chevy under the oaks, and the flatbed acts as a perfect makeshift standing table—one of my favorite "ranch tables." I arrange the food along the back, as a buffet, and everyone gathers around the sides. After sitting on a horse all day it feels nice to be on our feet for a while.

Everyone loosens their saddles and ties their horses to the sides of the trailers or trucks. I set the chips and dip out so people can start snacking, then hand out big cups of chili, and everyone crowds around to add cheese, hot sauce, and any other toppings they like. The chili is hearty and the corn bread is warm and fluffy. As we eat, I think of something my mom always says: that food always tastes especially good after a long day of hard work.

LAYERED AVOCADO DIP

ACTIVE TIME
10 minutes

TOTAL TIME
10 minutes

SERVES
8

1½ cups Tío's Beans
(page 25) or a 16-ounce
can refried beans

3 cups Guacamole
(page 123) or store-bought

2 cups Pico de Gallo
(page 21) or store-bought,
drained (see Tip)

3 cups sour cream

1 cup freshly grated
Cheddar or Monterey Jack

1 Roma tomato, cut into
½-inch dice

3 green onions, light green
parts only, thinly sliced

1 tablespoon roughly
chopped cilantro

Tortilla chips

Seven-layer dip is a favorite all over the country. The combination of flavorful beans, bright guacamole, tangy sour cream, cheese, tomatoes, and other fresh toppings is irresistible. While most layered dips follow the same basic method, every cook has their own favorite additions. My version sticks to the classic base ingredients, but I also top it with some thinly sliced green onions and fresh cilantro for a pop of flavor. While I prefer to make this dish with homemade beans, guacamole, and salsa, it's also great with ingredients from the market—and a fast crowd-pleaser.

Put the beans in a 9 × 9-inch casserole dish (or a medium bowl) and spread them to make an even layer. Add the guacamole in an even layer, followed by the pico de gallo and the sour cream, spreading each out evenly to fully cover the previous ingredient. Sprinkle the cheese on top, followed by the tomato, green onions, and cilantro. Refrigerate the dip until just before serving. Serve with tortilla chips.

TIP: Make sure to drain the pico before using it so that the dip doesn't get soupy.

RANCHERS' BEEF CHILI

ACTIVE TIME
25 minutes

TOTAL TIME
1 hour 25 minutes

SERVES
8 to 10

2 pounds chuck roast, at room temperature

Kosher salt

Ground black pepper

4 tablespoons extra virgin olive oil

1 onion, roughly chopped

2 garlic cloves, roughly chopped

2 teaspoons ground cumin

½ teaspoon chile powder

½ teaspoon smoked paprika

½ cup beer, ideally a lager or ale

One 14.5-ounce can diced fire-roasted tomatoes

One 15-ounce can red kidney beans, drained

One 15-ounce can garbanzo beans, drained

2 cups Bone Broth a.k.a. Beef Stock (page 85) or store-bought

Freshly grated queso fresco or Monterey Jack, chopped cilantro, and sliced green onions

Chili might just be the very best food to make for a crowd. It's filling and contains everything you want in a meal, from protein to fiber. It's also incredibly portable: you can make it ahead of time and reheat it anywhere from a friend's kitchen to a campsite. I make chili with cubes of meat rather than ground beef. This way, you end up with a variety of textures in the pot and you can actually taste all the individual ingredients as you eat. While this makes for a pretty hearty dish, I do make it year-round. We're close enough to the coast that we can get lots of fog in the evenings, even in summer, and it's nice to have something really satisfying to eat after a long day of work, no matter the time of year.

1. Cut the chuck roast into 1-inch cubes and use paper towels to pat the pieces dry. Season them generously with salt and pepper.

2. Heat 2 tablespoons of the olive oil in a large Dutch oven or heavy-duty pot over high heat. Lightly brown the meat on all sides, about 2 minutes per side. Remove the meat from the pot and set it aside.

3. Reduce the heat to medium. Add the remaining 2 tablespoons oil to the pot, then add the onion and garlic and 1 teaspoon of salt. Cook, stirring, until the onion is golden brown, about 5 minutes. Add the cumin, chile powder, and paprika to the pot and stir.

4. Add the beer and mix everything well. Bring the mixture to a simmer and cook until most of the beer has evaporated, about 2 minutes.

5. Put the beef back into the pot and add the canned tomatoes (and their liquid), both types of beans, and the broth.

6. Bring the mixture to a simmer and cook, partially covered, until the flavors have melded and the meat is fork-tender, at least 1 hour.

7. Serve with cheese, cilantro, and green onions.

BONE BROTH A.K.A. BEEF STOCK

ACTIVE TIME
30 mins

TOTAL TIME
4 to 24 hours

MAKES
about 2 quarts

3 pounds raw beef bones (such as knuckles, marrow bones, or neck bones)

2 medium yellow onions

1 garlic head

3 large carrots

2 to 3 ounces fresh ginger, roughly chopped (2 to 3 tablespoons)

3 bay leaves

1 tablespoon whole black peppercorns

1 tablespoon apple cider vinegar

1 teaspoon kosher salt

I like to make bone broth in big batches and freeze it, so it's ready for soups, chili (see page 83), and even cooking up rice or other grains. (It's also nice to drink on its own.) Roasting the bones before you make the broth really brings out their flavor, and adding apple cider vinegar (or any acid) to the water helps draw even more nutrients from the bones. I also add fresh ginger to my broths because it has a lot of health benefits.

The longer you cook this broth, the more flavor and nutrition you'll get out of the ingredients. You can leave this simmering on your stove all day—as long as you don't leave the house with the stove on! The finished broth may have a layer of fat sitting on the top; this has lots of flavor and nutrition, so don't discard all that good stuff!

1. Preheat the oven to 400°F.

2. Put the bones on a sheet pan and bake for 15 to 20 minutes, until you can hear the bones sizzling and they are light brown in color.

3. In the meantime, peel and quarter the onions, cut the head of garlic in half crosswise, and cut the carrots into 2-inch pieces.

4. Transfer everything from the sheet pan into a large Dutch oven or stockpot, making sure to scrape all the fat and little bits of meat off the pan for additional flavor. Add the onions, garlic, carrots, ginger, bay leaves, peppercorns, vinegar, and salt to the pot. Add 12 to 14 cups of water, enough so that the ingredients are covered by about 4 inches.

5. Cover the pot and bring the liquid to a gentle boil over medium heat. As soon as it boils, turn the heat down, so the broth is just simmering, then skim any excess fat and foam off the top. Continue simmering the stock, uncovered, for anywhere from 4 to 24 hours, adding more water if there is 2 inches or less above the top of the ingredients.

6. When the broth is done to your liking, strain it through a colander or sieve to remove the solids. Taste and adjust the seasoning. Let the broth cool a bit, then transfer it to a heatproof container and put it in the refrigerator to finish cooling. Use or freeze (in a freezer-safe container) within 3 days.

CAST-IRON CORN BREAD

ACTIVE TIME
10 minutes

TOTAL TIME
1 hour

SERVES
6 to 8

1 cup all-purpose flour

1 cup fine yellow cornmeal

½ cup granulated sugar

2 teaspoons baking powder

1 teaspoon kosher salt

1 cup reduced-fat buttermilk

2 large eggs

¼ cup vegetable oil

¾ cup fresh or frozen and thawed corn kernels

1 tablespoon unsalted butter

Honey Butter (optional; recipe follows)

My fluffy, tender, and slightly sweet corn bread is baked in a hot cast-iron pan so that the outer crust crisps up before the interior gets dry. I also like to serve it right from the pan. I don't generally like to add too many things to my corn bread, because I think the flavor is great on its own, but a handful of fresh corn kernels adds a nice pop of flavor to each bite.

1. Preheat the oven to 350°F.

2. Whisk the flour, cornmeal, sugar, baking powder, and salt together in a large bowl. Add the buttermilk and eggs and whisk well until combined, then whisk in the oil. Mix in the corn.

3. Melt the butter in a 10-inch cast-iron pan in the oven for 3 minutes. Carefully remove the pan from the oven and tip and rotate it so that the melted butter coats the bottom and sides. Pour the batter evenly into the hot pan.

4. Bake the corn bread for about 30 minutes, until a tester comes out moist but clean.

5. Let the corn bread cool for 10 minutes before serving with honey butter, if desired.

HONEY BUTTER

½ cup (1 stick) salted butter, at room temperature

2 tablespoons honey

ACTIVE TIME
5 minutes

TOTAL TIME
5 minutes

MAKES
½ cup

Mash the butter and honey together in a small bowl with a fork until they're well combined. Refrigerate until serving.

BIRTHDAY DINNER
IN THE LAVENDER FIELD

—————————————————

MY BIRTHDAY LANDS IN THE MIDDLE OF THE YEAR, RIGHT IN
the heart of summer. It's a beautiful season. The early-summer fog (known as "June gloom") has just ended, days are warm but not too hot, and the lavender field by my parents' house is just coming into full bloom.

When I was a kid, I always missed my friends by this part of the summer, so my parents would throw a big birthday party and invite everyone to the ranch. My dad would make a cloth flag decorated with my age and hang it on the willow tree in the front yard. Everyone would come—not only my friends but also their parents and siblings—and my mom would orchestrate classic children's games like red rover and let us run around in the garden and the fields near the house in our party clothes. These days, I still use my birthday as an opportunity to invite friends to the ranch.

ψ

I love planning a party. Being able to cook all my favorite foods and see people I love is my idea of a perfect day! Throughout my life, I've been lucky enough to meet some truly amazing women. I have circles of friends from childhood, high school, and college and women I became close to in those first few years of adulthood. Many of these dear friends now live all over the world, but they remain an incredibly important part of my day-to-day life. I make sure to stay in touch—to visit them when I can, invite them to the ranch, and just call whenever I need the kind of talk you can only have with someone you've known for years.

Tonight, I've invited some of my oldest friends to dinner. These women have known me for most of my life, they were all a part of my wedding, and we have supported each other for decades. We'll eat in the lavender field by my parents' house, right next to the spot where many of my childhood birthday parties took place, and take a break from our busy lives of work and family.

I've planned a meal inspired by the Italian side of my family. We'll start with fun cocktails and some appetizers: apricots stuffed with goat cheese and grilled peaches with burrata and prosciutto. For dinner, there will be two kinds of pastas, including one with homemade noodles, and a Caesar salad with big croutons. For dessert, we'll have a tall, four-layer chocolate cake—in my opinion, an absolutely essential part of any birthday party.

Because these women have known me for so long, they know that the party really starts with the cooking and the setup. So I'm not surprised when some of them call to ask if they can come early and help. The first to arrive is my friend and coauthor, Georgia, who is down visiting from Northern California. Georgia and I met on the first day of kindergarten and connected immediately. She even got married here, just a few yards from where we'll be having dinner. She helps me roll out the dough for spinach fettuccine, which I'll use to make a kind of summery take on pasta primavera. Katie arrives in full Katie style with a huge smile and a basketful of roses to decorate the cake. She gets to work setting up a table out by the lavender with help from Luz, who grew up on the ranch and is like a younger sister to me. When my cousins Roz and Julie arrive, they bring out plates and start to decorate. The last to arrive is Cáitrín, whom I met when our parents were working together; we spent much of our childhood waiting for our parents to get out of meetings.

Soon the food starts disappearing from our plates, and we're caught up telling old stories and sharing memories. By the time I cut everyone huge slices of cake, the weather has turned chilly, but no one seems to mind. Sweaters and coats come out, and we linger over dessert. It's rare that we can get together like this, without our kids and families and work to distract us, and we're going to stretch the evening out as long as possible.

The lavender is just beginning to peak at this time of year, and when we walk through the field, the breeze sends a light fragrance into the air. I'm glad we can take advantage of this moment in the season, because in a few weeks, my parents and brother will harvest and distill the flowers to make oil and hydrosol, which will be sold to artisans who make soaps and perfumes. Like everything on the ranch, the lavender serves a purpose. It's one of the many small agricultural investments my parents have made over the years to diversify our business. Keeping our life here sustainable means being willing to try out new things. This side business just happens to come with the added bonus of a gorgeous field of lavender—and I've been raised to believe that since we live at our work, we should take the time to enjoy its benefits whenever we can.

APRICOTS *with* GOAT CHEESE AND HONEY

ACTIVE TIME
15 minutes

TOTAL TIME
15 minutes

MAKES
24 apricot halves

12 apricots, halved lengthwise and pitted

4 ounces plain goat cheese (chèvre)

2 tablespoons whole milk

2 tablespoons honey

Maldon salt or other flaky sea salt

Fresh thyme (optional)

SPECIAL TOOLS

Pastry bag (optional)

Katie and I came up with this appetizer the first year we were doing Ranch Table events, because we had tons of apricots and needed to find a way to use them up and serve them to our guests (without just making lots and lots of galettes). Now we serve this at almost all our early-summer events, and it's always a huge hit. The mix of fruit, creamy cheese, honey, and sea salt gives these little bites a sweet-salty flavor, and putting a couple of fresh thyme leaves on each one rounds out the flavor in a really wonderful, unexpected way. They're particularly great for a party, because you can make them ahead of time and refrigerate them; just be sure to let them come up to room temperature before serving.

1. Set the apricot halves on a serving plate, cut side up.

2. Mix the cheese and milk together in a small bowl to smooth out and loosen up the texture of the cheese. Transfer the cheese mixture to the pastry bag or a plastic zip-top bag with a tip cut out of the corner.

3. Squeeze about 1 teaspoon of the cheese mixture into the cavity of each apricot half, creating a little mound. (Some will require more or less, depending on the size of the fruit.)

4. Drizzle the honey across the filled apricot halves, then top each one with a small pinch of salt and a couple of thyme leaves, if using.

GRILLED PEACHES *with* BURRATA AND PROSCIUTTO

ACTIVE TIME
30 minutes

TOTAL TIME
30 minutes

MAKES
8 peach halves

½ cup extra virgin olive oil, plus more for brushing

¼ cup freshly squeezed lemon juice

2 tablespoons finely chopped fresh mint, plus mint leaves for garnish

2 teaspoons honey

1 teaspoon Dijon mustard

½ teaspoon kosher salt

4 slightly firm medium peaches, halved lengthwise and pitted

One 8-ounce or two 4-ounce balls of burrata

8 thin prosciutto slices

The idea of cooking the peaches for this appetizer came about naturally: my family grills so often that we're always throwing unusual items onto the grate. Even the kids like to add things and help "invent" dishes. So one afternoon, I found myself cooking some slightly firm peaches. The heat caramelizes the fruit's sugars and gives it a bit of a char, making the peach both sweeter and slightly smoky. Add the creamy burrata and the rich and salty prosciutto and you have, basically, a perfect food. Serve it with a knife and fork.

1. Combine the olive oil, lemon juice, mint, honey, mustard, and salt in a small jar and shake well until the dressing looks creamy and thick.

2. Heat a wood or charcoal grill to high or a gas grill to medium. (If working with charcoal or wood, you should have very hot, white coals with only a few final flames; if you're using gas, the temperature should be about 350°F.)

3. Lightly brush the cut side of the peaches with olive oil.

4. Grill the peaches cut side down for about 5 minutes, until they have grill marks and the flesh is golden brown. Arrange them on a plate, grilled side up.

5. Place a spoonful of burrata in the cavity of a peach half (about one-eighth of an 8-ounce ball or one-fourth of a 4-ounce ball); there should be enough that the cheese mounds up, above the peach, and spills out of the cavity a bit. Fold a piece of prosciutto in half and place it on top of the mound of cheese. Repeat with the remaining grilled peaches. Pour 2 tablespoons of the dressing over each filled peach. Garnish with mint leaves.

TIP: If you don't want to heat a grill for this recipe, you can cook the peaches cut side up under the broiler, close to the flame, until they start to turn golden brown.

RIGATONI *with* SAUSAGE, EGGPLANT, BASIL, AND MOZZARELLA

ACTIVE TIME
1 hour 20 minutes

TOTAL TIME
1 hour 20 minutes

SERVES
6 to 8

2 medium Italian eggplants
(1½ pounds)

1 tablespoon plus 2½
teaspoons kosher salt

1 pound mild Italian
sausage

1 pound spicy Italian
sausage

1 large red bell pepper

1 pound dried rigatoni

½ cup plus 3 tablespoons
extra virgin olive oil, plus
more as needed

1 large yellow onion,
roughly chopped

4 large garlic cloves,
roughly chopped

8 ounces low-moisture
mozzarella

3 cups Quick Marinara
(page 99) or store-bought

1 cup roughly chopped
basil leaves

This classic Italian American dish has been one of my favorites since I was a kid. I first had it at an old Italian restaurant my parents and I used to go to in Santa Barbara, on a Friday evening after school and work. Once I started cooking for myself, I re-created it in my kitchen because the combination of flavors—sausage, eggplant, and big pieces of mozzarella all dressed with marinara—is really comforting.

1. Cut the eggplant crosswise into 1-inch-thick slices. Lay the slices on a plate and sprinkle them on one side with ½ tablespoon of the salt, then let the slices rest for 10 minutes. Blot the slices with a paper towel to remove the moisture that has beaded on top. Flip the slices over and repeat the salting, resting, and blotting process with another ½ tablespoon of the salt. Cut the slices into roughly 1-inch dice.

2. In the meantime, cut both types of sausage into 1-inch-thick slices. Deseed the bell pepper, then cut it into ½-inch-thick strips and cut the strips into 1-inch-long pieces.

3. Fill a large pot with water, add 2 teaspoons of the salt, and bring the water to a boil over high heat. Add the rigatoni and cook until the pasta is al dente according to the package instructions, then drain.

4. In the meantime, heat 1 tablespoon of the olive oil in a very large cast-iron pan or a Dutch oven over medium heat. Add the sausage and cook it, flipping once or twice, until it is cooked through and browned on both sides, about 10 minutes. Use a slotted spoon to transfer the sausage chunks to a medium bowl, leaving the fat in the pan. Set the sausage aside.

5. Add the onion, bell pepper, and garlic to the pan along with 2 more tablespoons of the olive oil. Season with ¼ teaspoon of the salt and cook over medium heat, stirring occasionally but letting the pieces brown, until the pepper is tender, about 10 minutes. Use the slotted spoon to scoop the vegetables into the same bowl as the sausage, leaving the oil in the pan.

continued

6. Reduce the heat to medium-low and add the diced eggplant squares to the pan. Pour the remaining ½ cup olive oil over them and stir to thoroughly coat all the pieces. (The eggplant will soak up most of the oil quickly.) Season the eggplant with the remaining ¼ teaspoon salt and cook it, stirring occasionally. If some pieces are still white, meaning they haven't soaked up oil in the first couple of minutes of cooking, drizzle more oil onto those pieces as necessary. They will turn yellow as they absorb the oil.

7. Cook the eggplant until very brown and very soft and some sides are crispy, about 15 minutes. Use the spatula or slotted spoon to transfer them to the bowl with the other cooked ingredients. Turn the heat off but leave the pan on the stove.

8. Cut the mozzarella into ½-inch-thick slices, and then cut the slices into approximately 1-inch pieces; set it aside.

9. Add the marinara to the pan with the leftover oil and heat it over low heat until it is just hot, then return the sausage and vegetable mixture to the pan and stir to coat everything well.

10. Put the pasta and the sauce into the pot you boiled the pasta in and mix everything together. Add the mozzarella and mix well as it begins to melt so that the pieces don't stick together. Add the basil, mix well, and serve hot.

QUICK MARINARA

ACTIVE TIME
20 minutes

TOTAL TIME
35 minutes

MAKES
4 cups

¼ cup extra virgin olive oil

1 medium yellow or sweet onion, cut into ½-inch dice

3 large garlic cloves, roughly chopped

1 tablespoon kosher salt, plus more as needed

6 pounds tomatoes (ideally a mix of Roma and other varieties), cut into ½-inch dice

1 tablespoon granulated sugar

½ cup basil leaves, roughly chopped

Growing up, I often watched my mom make homemade marinara. Her pasta dishes are some of my favorite foods in the world, and a good marinara sauce is a key ingredient in most of them. Now I, too, spend a few evenings making my own sauce every summer. I usually toss a jar or two right into the fridge and use it for pasta that week, then can the rest. That way I can open it up on cold winter nights and let the flavors transport me straight to the summer garden with its orderly rows of heirloom tomatoes, onions, garlic, and basil; it also freezes well. This recipe makes 1 quart of sauce, but you can easily multiply the ingredients and make a lot more to keep for later in the year.

1. Heat the olive oil in a Dutch oven or heavy-duty pot over medium heat, then add the onion, garlic, and salt. Cook, stirring occasionally, until the onion is translucent and beginning to brown, about 10 minutes.

2. Add the tomatoes to the pot and bring the mixture to a simmer. Cook the tomatoes, stirring occasionally and crushing any particularly large pieces with a wooden spoon, until they start to fall apart, about 5 minutes.

3. Add the sugar and stir until it dissolves. Cover the pot, reduce the heat to low, and cook the sauce until everything has really melded and the sauce has thickened a bit, about 15 minutes.

4. Transfer the sauce to a blender and process it until smooth. Add the basil, then taste and adjust the seasoning.

5. Transfer the sauce to a heatproof jar and refrigerate. Use or freeze (in a freezer-safe container) within a few days.

FETTUCCINE *with* ROASTED SUMMER VEGETABLES

ACTIVE TIME
15 minutes

TOTAL TIME
45 minutes

SERVES
4 to 6

2 medium zucchini
(2 pounds)

2 pounds cherry tomatoes

8 garlic cloves

4 large ears sweet corn

¾ cup extra virgin olive oil,
plus more to taste

1 tablespoon plus
2 teaspoons kosher salt,
plus more to taste

½ teaspoon ground black
pepper, plus more to taste

Homemade Fettuccine
(page 102) or 1 pound dried
store-bought

Freshly grated Parmesan
(optional)

I like to make this dish at the height of summer, because it's a great way to really enjoy the flavors of all the produce in our garden in one dish. Instead of spending time cooking everything on the stove, I roast all the vegetables on sheet pans, which frees me up to do other things. It also has the added benefit of keeping each ingredient's flavor really pure, so you can taste the different vegetables in the finished dish. If I can, I prefer to use Sungold cherry tomatoes, because they have a wonderful, sweet flavor and a beautiful golden-orange color. The result is bright and colorful and tastes like all the best parts of summer.

1. Preheat the oven to 400°F.

2. Cut the zucchini in half lengthwise, then slice them crosswise into ½-inch-thick half moons. Put them in a large bowl along with the tomatoes. Mash the garlic with the side of the knife to break the cloves into large pieces, then add them to the bowl. Cut the kernels off the corn ears and add them to the bowl with the vegetables. Add the olive oil, 1 tablespoon of the salt, and the pepper and mix everything well.

3. Divide the vegetables between two sheet pans and roast them until tender, about 30 minutes.

4. While the vegetables are roasting, fill a large pot with water, add the remaining 2 teaspoons salt, and bring the water to a boil over high heat. When the vegetables are almost cooked, boil the pasta for 5 minutes (or the time called for on the package).

5. Drain the pasta and transfer it to a bowl. Top the pasta with the vegetables, toss everything, and add a bit more olive oil, salt, and pepper if needed, as well as the Parmesan cheese, if using.

HOMEMADE FETTUCCINE

ACTIVE TIME
45 minutes

TOTAL TIME
*1 hour 15 minutes
(1 hour 35 minutes if
you let the pasta rest)*

MAKES
about 1 pound

2 cups all-purpose flour,
plus about ½ cup for
kneading and more for
dusting

4 large eggs, at room
temperature

Semolina flour, for dusting
the pasta (or additional all-
purpose flour)

SPECIAL TOOLS

Pasta roller (optional)

I love making homemade pasta. It's really simple—it takes only about 30 minutes—and it gives you such a light and fresh texture. Sometimes I also add a bit of cooked spinach to the dough to give it a fun green color (as I've done here; see the variation on page 104). Pasta is also an easy project to get the kids involved in, and they have a great time rolling the dough through the pasta maker. I use a countertop pasta maker with a hand crank. If you don't have a pasta maker, you can follow these same instructions using a rolling pin, then cut the sheets into strips with a knife. If you use a rolling pin, you'll need to let the dough rest for 20 minutes before rolling it out, so that the gluten relaxes.

1. Pour the flour onto a clean surface. Form it into a mound, then make a well in the center that is large enough to fit all 4 eggs (a). Crack the eggs into the well (b).

2. Carefully whisk the eggs with a fork, whisking in the flour little by little (c), starting with the flour that forms the walls of the well and working outward until everything is mixed into a shaggy mass.

3. Knead and fold the dough to incorporate the last of the flour (using a bench scraper or a butter knife to gather the ingredients together), then knead the dough, turning it as you go, for 8 to 10 minutes, dusting the surface with more flour when you feel the dough is sticking to your hands or the surface. The dough should be soft, smooth, and elastic.

4. Make the dough into a log and cover it with plastic wrap or a clean damp cloth. If using a rolling pin to make the noodles, set an overturned bowl on top of the log (so that the dough doesn't dry out) and let it rest for about 20 minutes.

5. Using the pasta machine (or a rolling pin and a floured surface), roll out your noodles: Divide the dough into 8 pieces (d), keeping the pieces covered until they're needed. Working with one piece at a time, roll it through the widest setting on the pasta machine (or roll it out with a rolling pin until it's ⅛ inch thick). Fold the dough into thirds, like a letter (e), and pass it back through the machine (or roll it out) again; make sure to feed it into the machine with one of the open sides going into the rollers first, so that any air bubbles can escape out the other side. Repeat this process two more times; the dough should be pliable and stretchy.

continued

6. Adjust the pasta machine to the next thinnest setting and pass the dough through. If the dough starts to feel sticky, add flour so that it doesn't get stuck in the machine. Continue adjusting the settings and rolling the dough through, so that it gets thinner and thinner (f), until you've rolled it out on the #6 setting (or roll it with a rolling pin until you can just start to see the shape and shadow of your hand through the dough). Lay the rolled sheet of dough onto a surface dusted with semolina flour (or all-purpose flour).

7. Repeat the rolling process with the remaining pieces of dough.

8. Attach the fettuccine cutter to your pasta maker. Working with one at a time, pass the pasta sheets through the cutter. (If you don't have a pasta machine, you can cut the fettuccine with a sharp knife.) Dust the noodles with a bit of semolina flour to keep them from sticking, and let them sit while you make your sauce if using them fresh. If you prefer to dry your pasta, hang it up (over a clean dowel, clothes hangers, or the back of chairs covered with clean cloths), set it in an area away from the sun, and allow it to dry until it snaps when broken, 12 to 24 hours. Dried pasta can be stored at room temperature, in an airtight container, for a few days.

9. Boil the pasta in salted water until al dente; it takes 5 minutes to cook whether it's fresh or dried.

VARIATION: SPINACH PASTA

To give your pasta a nice green hue (and add more nutrition), sauté ¼ pound of fresh spinach with 1 tablespoon extra virgin olive oil, squeeze it to remove any liquid, then chop it very finely. Add it to the eggs in the flour well in step 2. Make the rest of the recipe as instructed; you'll likely have to add extra flour when dusting the counter in step 3.

CAESAR SALAD *with* HOMEMADE CROUTONS

ACTIVE TIME
10 minutes

TOTAL TIME
40 minutes

SERVES
4 to 6

FOR THE CROUTONS

½ pound French bread

½ cup extra virgin olive oil

1 tablespoon fresh thyme

1 teaspoon kosher salt

⅛ teaspoon ground black pepper

FOR THE DRESSING

2 anchovy fillets

2 garlic cloves, smashed

¾ cup extra virgin olive oil

3 tablespoons freshly squeezed lemon juice

1 tablespoon Dijon mustard

½ teaspoon kosher salt

¼ teaspoon ground black pepper

1 cup freshly grated Parmesan

FOR THE SALAD

2 romaine lettuce hearts

1 cup freshly grated Parmesan

You can never go wrong with a Caesar salad. I make my dressing without the egg yolk that you find in many recipes so that I can prepare it in advance and serve it at big events or picnics without worrying about it going bad. Instead, I use a bit of extra Dijon mustard to add some creaminess. I also like to make my own croutons. It's a great way to use up extra bread, especially because croutons are best when made with slightly stale bread. They add lots of great crunch, and I love how I end up with croutons in lots of different sizes.

MAKE THE CROUTONS

1. Preheat the oven to 350°F.

2. Cut the bread into 1-inch cubes. Place the cubes in a large bowl, drizzle them with the olive oil, and toss them with your hands until all the pieces are coated. Add the thyme, salt, and pepper and toss until the seasonings are evenly distributed.

3. Spread the croutons out on a sheet pan and bake them for about 15 minutes, until they're golden brown. Use a metal spatula to flip the croutons, then bake them for another 15 minutes, until they're golden brown all over and crunchy; set them aside to cool.

MAKE THE DRESSING

Put the anchovies, garlic, olive oil, lemon juice, mustard, salt, pepper, and Parmesan in a food processor and process until smooth.

ASSEMBLE THE SALAD

Cut the romaine crosswise into 1- to 2-inch-thick ribbons. Toss the romaine with the dressing in a large bowl. Add the Parmesan and the croutons and toss everything together gently. Serve immediately.

EASY FOUR-LAYER CHOCOLATE CAKE *with* FRESH STRAWBERRIES

ACTIVE TIME
50 minutes

TOTAL TIME
*2 hours 5 minutes,
including cooling*

SERVES
8 to 10

Vegetable shortening, for greasing

2½ cups cake flour, plus more for the pans

1 cup natural unsweetened cocoa powder

2 teaspoons baking soda

½ teaspoon kosher salt

1 cup (2 sticks) unsalted butter, at room temperature

1 cup granulated sugar

1 cup packed light brown sugar

2 large eggs

1 teaspoon pure vanilla extract

1½ cups reduced-fat buttermilk

1 cup hot coffee

Chocolate Cream Cheese Frosting (recipe follows)

I'm a gal who loves chocolate. If I get a choice of what kind of dessert to have, I'm always going to go with the chocolate option, no matter what else is on the menu. So it's not surprising that I have a chocolate cake for pretty much all my birthdays. My mom's mother, "Nana," made beautiful cakes, and when she lived with us, she made the cakes for every celebration. She insisted on using cake flour, which is lighter than all-purpose flour and gives you a more tender crumb. I follow her lead, but you can use all-purpose flour if that's what you have; just know that your cake will be a little bit denser and heavier.

---

1. Preheat the oven to 350°F.

2. Grease the cake pans with vegetable shortening. Line the bottoms with parchment paper circles, then grease the top of the parchment. Pour about 1 tablespoon of flour into each pan and tip the pans to coat them, then tap out the excess.

3. Sift the flour, cocoa powder, baking soda, and salt into a medium bowl.

4. Put the butter and both sugars into the bowl of a stand mixer fitted with the paddle attachment or a large bowl (if using a hand mixer) and cream them together on medium speed until light and fluffy, 3 minutes. Add the eggs one at a time, beating the mixture on medium speed between each addition until it is fully mixed in, about 30 seconds. Add the vanilla and beat until everything is just mixed.

5. Add one-third of the flour-cocoa mixture to the mixer and mix on low until it is just incorporated. Add half the buttermilk and mix until it is just incorporated. Repeat until you've used all the flour-cocoa mixture and buttermilk, ending with the last one-third of the dry ingredients. Scrape the bottom of the bowl to ensure that all ingredients are well combined. Last, add the coffee and mix just until it is incorporated.

6. Divide the batter between the prepared cake pans and smooth the tops with a rubber spatula.

continued

1 pound strawberries, hulled and sliced, plus whole strawberries for decorating

Edible flowers, such as rose, lavender, jasmine, and calendula

SPECIAL TOOLS

Two 9-inch-round cake pans

7. Bake the cakes for 30 to 45 minutes, until a tester inserted into the center comes out moist but clean (begin testing at 25 minutes, to be safe). Let the cakes cool in the pans for 1 hour, then carefully flip them onto racks to finish cooling to room temperature.

8. When the cakes have cooled, use a serrated knife to cut the layers in half horizontally, to make four thinner layers. Reserve one of the bottom layers to use on the top of the cake.

9. Spread a small dollop of frosting on a serving plate to hold the cake in place. Put one cake layer on the plate and press it down gently so it adheres. Add 1 cup of frosting to the top of the cake layer and use an offset spatula or a butter knife to spread it out evenly all the way to the edges. Pat one-third of the sliced strawberries with paper towels to remove excess moisture, then lay them on the frosting, starting by making a ring around the outside of the cake and then scattering the remaining pieces across the rest of the frosting.

10. Repeat this process two more times, using another cake layer, another cup of frosting, and another one-third of the berries each time.

11. Put the reserved final layer of cake on top; invert it so that you have a flat, even surface on the top of the cake. Spread more frosting on this top layer, then spread the remaining frosting along the sides of the cake.

12. Refrigerate the cake until the frosting sets and is firm, about 1 hour, then decorate it with the whole berries and the flowers.

TIP: When I make a chocolate cake, I often like to prep the pan with cocoa powder instead of flour because there's no such thing as too much chocolate!

CHOCOLATE CREAM CHEESE FROSTING

4 ounces semisweet chocolate, roughly chopped

Three 8-ounce packages cream cheese, at room temperature

1 cup (2 sticks) unsalted butter, at room temperature

4 cups powdered sugar, sifted

¼ teaspoon kosher salt

ACTIVE TIME
15 minutes

TOTAL TIME
45 minutes

MAKES
*about 5 cups
(enough for 1 cake)*

1. Melt the chocolate in a double boiler (or a large heatproof bowl set over a pot of simmering water) over medium heat, stirring frequently with a rubber spatula. Remove the melted chocolate from the heat; set it aside.

2. Put the cream cheese and butter in the bowl of a stand mixer fitted with the paddle attachment and cream them on medium speed until they're well mixed, about 1 minute.

3. Increase the mixer speed to medium-high and slowly add the melted chocolate. Continue beating the mixture until everything is well combined, then scrape the sides and bottom of the bowl and beat again.

4. Add the powdered sugar to the mixer 1 cup at a time, mixing after each addition to incorporate it. Add the salt and beat until just combined. Use a rubber spatula to finish mixing, making sure everything is well incorporated and there are no streaks.

5. Refrigerate the frosting until it firms up a little and holds its shape but is still easy to spread, about 30 minutes.

6. Frost the cake as directed in the recipe.

MINT LEMONADE

ACTIVE TIME
10 minutes

TOTAL TIME
30 minutes

SERVES
8 to 10

1 cup granulated sugar

1 cup loosely packed mint leaves

5 cups water

½ cup freshly squeezed lemon juice

Ice cubes

We always make a ton of lemonade whenever we have an event or party. We even have a couple of big glass dispensers—the kind with a little metal spigot on the bottom—to serve it in. I like adding mint to our lemonade during the spring and summer, because I grow it in my garden, and it's basically impossible to kill mint—it will take over your garden if you're not careful!—so I need to find ways to use it up. The good news is that it adds a really refreshing flavor to the lemonade and makes it feel a little extra special.

1. Combine the sugar, mint leaves, and 1 cup of the water in a small saucepan and bring the mixture to a simmer over medium heat. Continue simmering, stirring occasionally, until the mint darkens and wilts and the mixture turns light green, about 5 minutes. Remove the mixture from the heat and let it cool to room temperature, about 20 minutes, then strain it through a fine-mesh sieve to remove the mint. This is a mint simple syrup.

2. Pour the simple syrup into a large pitcher and add the lemon juice and the remaining 4 cups water. Stir the lemonade, then add enough ice to fill the pitcher.

LAVENDER BEE'S KNEES

ACTIVE TIME
2 minutes

TOTAL TIME
2 minutes

MAKES
1 drink

Ice cubes

1½ ounces gin

1 ounce freshly squeezed lemon juice

1 ounce Lavender Honey Simple Syrup (recipe follows)

Dried culinary lavender head (optional)

SPECIAL TOOLS

Cocktail shaker with a strainer

The bee's knees is one of my favorite Prohibition-era cocktails because its sweet flavor comes from honey—and I love an excuse to put honey in anything. In this version, I've added another of my favorite flavors: lavender. I get my lavender right from the field by my parents' house, and I like to make this drink around the time we're harvesting the flowers. The harvest always seems like it happens during the hottest week of the year, and it's a ton of work. After a long day in the sun, it's fun to create something delicious with some of the blossoms we've picked. (You can use either fresh or dried lavender for this recipe.)

Fill a cocktail shaker with ice. Add the gin, lemon juice, and honey syrup to the shaker and shake for 30 seconds. Strain the liquid into a chilled cocktail glass and garnish with the dried lavender, if using.

LAVENDER HONEY SIMPLE SYRUP

½ cup honey

½ cup water

5 to 10 culinary lavender heads (fresh or dried)

ACTIVE TIME
5 minutes

TOTAL TIME
25 minutes

MAKES
1 cup

Combine the honey, water, and lavender in a small saucepan and bring the mixture to a simmer over medium heat. Continue simmering, stirring occasionally, for 5 minutes. Remove the syrup from the heat and let it cool to room temperature, about 20 minutes, then strain the mixture through a fine-mesh sieve to remove the lavender. Store the syrup in the refrigerator for up to 1 week.

FIESTA FAMILY REUNION

GUACAMOLE · 123

BEEF EMPANADAS · 125

MERCEDES'S ENCHILADAS · 129

PORK RIBS STEAMED IN APPLE CIDER · 131

GRILLED ANAHEIMS WITH GARLIC SALT · 133

CHILE RELLENO CASSEROLE · 135

TOMATO SALAD WITH CORN AND KALAMATA OLIVES · 137

SPANISH RICE · 138

RED WINE SANGRIA · 141

BLACKBERRY MARGARITA · 143

with Blackberry Simple Syrup 143

"VIVA LA FIESTA!" JACK YELLS AS HE CRACKS AN EGG ON

my head. I feel the hard, startling smack, then there's confetti everywhere, falling down my face and my hair. I jump up and grab a colorful painted egg from our basket, and Jack runs away, shrieking with laughter.

The first week of August marks Santa Barbara's largest festival, Old Spanish Days, or Fiesta. For five days, the whole city comes together to celebrate the area's history with dancing, music, street fairs, and parades. The celebrations start Wednesday evening, on the steps of the Old Mission of Santa Barbara. A huge crowd gathers on the grassy lawn to watch flamenco, folklórico, and Native Chumash performers do traditional dances and to listen to mariachi bands fronted by young children who sing with so much joy and passion that everyone cheers in appreciation.

When I was growing up, I belonged to a flamenco company that danced on these very steps. My parents and I ran from performance to performance, hauling my long, ruffled, lace dresses with us, so that I could dance sevillanas and alegrías, then enjoy some tacos and grilled corn covered with mayonnaise, chile, lime, and cheese. We also bought tons of cascarones—painted eggs filled with confetti that everyone enjoys smashing on each other's heads.

I studied flamenco for many years, and it has always been a huge part of my life, but these days my family is more focused on the rodeos that take place throughout the week. My boys dress in their crispest Wranglers and cowboy hats and stand up in their seats, excited at the skill of the ropers and horses. When Jack was six, he talked me into letting him enter his first "mutton busting" competition, an event where kids see who can ride a sheep the longest, and he won his first set of spurs.

♈

Fiesta is also a time of celebration for my extended family. Cousins come from across the country to celebrate, and we hold a big family reunion at the ranch the weekend before the festivities begin. My mom and my cousin Julie's mom, Delfina, started this tradition back in the 1980s, when they realized that many of the second and third cousins didn't really know each other anymore, and it's been a highlight of every year since. The gathering is an opportunity to discuss the business of the ranch—the work we're doing and plans for the future—but it's mostly a way to keep everyone connected across the generations. Families from as far away as New Mexico, Arizona, and Wyoming come stay in the Casa for the weekend, sleeping among the portraits of our ancestors and the old furniture and books that they've left behind, and spend their days hiking, going to nearby beaches, and reconnecting with other family members and with the land.

The big event of the weekend is a lunch under the arbor, which is covered in grapevines at this time of year. Everyone chips in to help cook the meal. When I arrive in the late morning, things are already in full swing. Our cousin Billy King is at the grill cooking sausages and a dozen tri-tips, and some of my dad's second cousins are telling stories about how they used to march in the Fiesta parade with the actor Leo Carrillo when they were kids.

Others are grilling chiles at a portable grill at the end of the picnic tables, and half a dozen people have gathered around and are peeling and seeding the charred peppers. When the chiles have been prepared, we'll dress them with a little bit of oil and some garlic salt and pile them on the tri-tip— and on pretty much everything else we eat. Some of the massive pile of chiles also goes in some simple grilled quesadillas as a snack for everyone.

A group of teenagers with purple or pink hair have formed a little crew of their own and are gathered at the other end of the tables, putting flowers from the garden into cans to decorate the tables. When the flowers are done, they retreat to the old covered porch to continue their competitive game of Uno. From the outside, the girls look like a group of close friends—they clearly have similar interests and styles and move in a pack—but they're actually all distant cousins. My boys have also found all the kids about their age, and that group has taken off to explore nearby forts and climb trees.

As lunchtime approaches, more and more family members start to arrive. My brother, Justin, arrives with my parents and helps set up the buffet table. In addition to our cousins, we also invite neighbors and other families who live on the ranch or work with us in some way, and I'm happy to see our beekeeper, Billy Williams; Eric, the ranch's lawyer, who is really like family; and Bruce and Sydni, historical contractors who have helped restore many parts of the Casa.

When the food is ready, the kids ring the dinner bell, and everyone lines up at the buffet. Everyone brings something to share, and in addition to the tri-tips and chiles, we have a whole table full of wonderful salads and roast vegetables, beans, corn on the cob, rice, and garlic bread. I bring out a big platter of ribs and my mom brings a chile relleno casserole and classic family dishes: beef empanadas and cheese-and-onion enchiladas with a homemade red chile sauce. These recipes have been passed down in our family for generations, and my mom and I always make them for these kinds of special occasions.

During lunch, some of the older family members begin telling stories about their parents' generation. They talk about how Frederika, my grandfather's sister, was born on the day the Wright brothers first flew, and how my great-uncle Dibbs used to call the old sycamore tree growing by the arbor his "brother," because it was planted the year he was born.

I've just finished eating when three-year-old Tatum walks over. This is her first trip to the ranch, but she already knows what to expect, and she's looking forward to one thing: "When we going to hit the pitata?" she asks, her eyes wide. The piñata that marks the end of the meal at these reunions is the kids' favorite part of the day, and it looks like they've found the cutest possible messenger to encourage me to set it up. I give in easily and grab Austin to help me swing a rope over a branch on the sycamore. I love how much fun everyone has with such a simple party activity—not just the kids but also the rest of the family gathered around and taking photos and laughing.

We line the kids up from youngest to oldest, from three to fourteen, and everyone is full of jitters and excitement. Once tiny Tatum has had a chance to get in a few whacks, we start blindfolding the kids and spinning them around. My goal is to let the kids actually hit the piñata but to also keep it reasonably whole long enough for even the oldest to get a turn. After the last of the teenagers gives the now-torn and broken ball of cardboard and crepe paper a good final whack, Roz shakes the candy all over the ground so that the kids don't end up in one big dogpile, and then we stand back and watch the rush. The sweetest thing is seeing how the older kids hand candy to the little ones, making sure everyone has enough. In the end, the "pitata" is a huge success, and everyone comes away happy with their haul.

The kids form a circle and start trading their loot, and I hover on the edges, discreetly watching them talk and tease and laugh together. Some of these cousins won't see each other for a whole year, but it won't matter. This place, and these shared memories, are enough to bond them to the ranch and to one another. These family reunions are the reason I'm so close with my cousins today, and now we're making sure we give that same gift of connection to the next generation, passing down our belief in the importance of family and tradition.

GUACAMOLE

ACTIVE TIME
10 minutes

TOTAL TIME
10 minutes

MAKES
about 3 cups

6 medium avocados

1 Roma tomato, finely diced

1 small white onion, finely chopped

1 teaspoon kosher salt, plus more to taste

4 to 6 tablespoons freshly squeezed lime juice, plus more to taste

We can't grow avocados on the ranch because it gets too cold in the winter this far inland, but we have neighbors a few miles closer to the coast (where it's warmer) who have trees. I like the flavor of Hass avocados, rather than green-skinned bacon avocados, another variety that also grows well in this area. Any guacamole recipe is really just a list of ingredients and a method—you never know how much flesh your avocados will have, how much fat they'll have in them, or how tart your limes will be, and all these factors will affect the overall flavor of the dish. So start with the amounts listed below, but make sure to taste and adjust the quantities and seasonings as you go.

1. Scoop the avocados into a medium bowl and cut them with two butter knives until you have small pieces.

2. Add the tomato, onion, and salt and stir to mix. Add about half the lime juice and mix, then taste the guacamole and continue adding more lime juice and salt as needed until you've reached a flavor you like.

3. Serve the guacamole immediately or cover it, pressing plastic wrap right onto the surface to keep it from browning in the refrigerator.

BEEF EMPANADAS

ACTIVE TIME

1 hour 50 minutes

TOTAL TIME

6 hours 20 minutes, including resting and chilling

MAKES

about 24 empanadas

FOR THE FILLING

½ cup extra virgin olive oil

1 pound beef brisket or chuck steak

1½ teaspoons kosher salt

¼ teaspoon ground black pepper

6 cups Bone Broth a.k.a. Beef Stock (page 85) or store-bought, plus more as needed

1 large white onion, minced

1 teaspoon chili powder

1 tablespoon finely chopped fresh oregano leaves

2 teaspoons ground cumin

1 cup raisins

½ cup canned sliced black olives, drained

½ cup dry sherry

¼ cup granulated sugar

¼ cup pine nuts

Crisp, crunchy Spanish empanadas filled with raisin-studded, chile-scented beef have been part of our family's cooking traditions for generations. The filling includes two important ingredients (pine nuts and olives) that mark the foods of the Californios, Spanish-speaking people who came to Alta California from Mexico (during and just after the colonial era). "If you see olives, you know it's a Californio recipe," my mom likes to say. The combination is so delicious that we make these treats for all our big family celebrations.

START THE FILLING

Preheat the oven to 300°F. Heat ¼ cup of the olive oil in a Dutch oven or heavy-duty pot on the stove over medium-high heat. Season the beef with 1 teaspoon of the salt and the pepper. Brown the beef on all sides, 8 to 10 minutes total. Remove the beef from the pot, then drain away most of the excess fat, leaving only 2 tablespoons in the pot. Return the beef to the pot, then add the broth, adding as much as is necessary to make sure the meat is fully submerged. Cover the pot and braise the meat in the oven for about 2½ hours, until fork-tender.

MAKE THE DOUGH

Combine the flour, butter, and salt in a large bowl and, using your fingers, rub the butter into the flour until pea-size crumbles form. Add the warm water and stir until a dough forms. Turn the dough out onto a lightly floured surface and knead it until it is fairly smooth, about 4 minutes. Wrap the dough in plastic wrap and refrigerate it for at least 1 hour.

FINISH THE FILLING

1. When the beef is done, remove it from the oven and let it sit in the pot until cool enough to handle, about 30 minutes. Transfer the beef to a cutting board, reserving 1 cup of the cooking liquid. Use two forks to shred the meat into thin strands, then finely chop it.

2. Clean the pot and wipe it dry. Add the remaining ¼ cup olive oil and heat it over medium-high heat; add the onion and the remaining ½ teaspoon salt and cook, stirring, until golden brown, 8 to 10 minutes. Add the chili powder, oregano, and cumin and cook, stirring, until the spices are fragrant, 1 minute.

continued

FOR THE DOUGH

4 cups all-purpose flour, plus more for dusting

6 tablespoons (¾ stick) cold unsalted butter, cubed

1½ teaspoons kosher salt

1½ cups water

Canola oil

¼ cup granulated sugar

SPECIAL TOOLS

4-inch biscuit cutter

Deep-fry thermometer

3. Add the beef and the reserved cooking liquid, along with the raisins, olives, sherry, sugar, and pine nuts. Bring the mixture to a boil, then reduce the heat to medium, partially cover the pot, and cook, stirring occasionally, until the raisins are plump and the meat has absorbed most of the liquid, 15 to 20 minutes. Let the filling cool to room temperature, about 30 minutes.

MAKE THE EMPANADAS

1. Divide the dough in half and place one half onto a lightly floured surface; cover the remaining dough with a damp kitchen towel. Roll the dough out to ¼ to ⅛ inch thick. Use the biscuit cutter to cut out 12 circles of dough. Roll each circle with a rolling pin to about 5 inches in diameter. Brush the edges of the circles with a little bit of water and place 2 tablespoons of filling in the center of each. Fold the disks in half, to form half moons, and use the tines of a fork to crimp and seal the edges, making sure there is no air trapped in the center. Repeat with the other half of the dough and the remaining filling.

2. Set the empanadas on two sheet pans lined with parchment paper and refrigerate them for about 30 minutes to let the dough firm up.

3. Pour 2 inches of canola oil into a clean Dutch oven or heavy-duty pot, attach a deep-fry thermometer, and heat the oil over medium-high heat until the thermometer reads 350°F. Working in batches, fry the empanadas, flipping them once or twice, until they are crunchy and golden, about 5 minutes. Transfer them to trays lined with paper towels to drain and immediately sprinkle them lightly with some of the sugar.

TIP: You can double or triple this recipe and freeze the uncooked empanadas. Fry the frozen empanadas until crunchy and golden, 6 to 7 minutes.

MERCEDES'S ENCHILADAS

ACTIVE TIME
1 hour

TOTAL TIME
1 hour 40 minutes

SERVES
4 to 6

10 dried Anaheim or New Mexican chiles

6 dried pasilla chiles

3 cups boiling water

4 garlic cloves

5 tablespoons extra virgin olive oil

5 tablespoons all-purpose flour

1 tablespoon apple cider vinegar

2 teaspoons dried oregano

½ teaspoon kosher salt

3 tablespoons extra virgin olive oil

2 large yellow onions, thinly sliced

Eight 6-inch flour tortillas

10 ounces queso fresco or other salty, melty cheese, crumbled

One 6-ounce can large pitted black olives, drained and roughly chopped

Years ago, my mom went through my dad's family's old notebooks and translated my great-grandmother Mercedes's handwritten cookbooks from Spanish to English. One of the recipes from that collection was for these simple enchiladas made with just caramelized onions and cheese. The recipe also calls for black olives, an ingredient that you see in many dishes made by the Californios. But the real star of the dish is the chile sauce. Once you see how easy it is, you won't want to go back to store-bought sauce again! (I suggest wearing plastic gloves when working with chiles because they can irritate your skin.)

1. Put both types of chiles in a large bowl, cover them with the boiling water, and put a cloth or plate over the bowl to trap in the heat. Let the chiles sit until soft, about 20 minutes. Strain the chiles, reserving 2½ cups of the soaking liquid.

2. Remove the stems and most of the seeds from the chiles. Transfer the soft chiles to a blender and add the reserved soaking liquid and the garlic. Puree until smooth.

3. Heat the olive oil in a medium saucepan over medium heat. Add the flour and cook, whisking constantly, until it takes on a light caramel color, about 3 minutes. Add the chile puree, vinegar, oregano, and ¼ teaspoon of the salt to the pot. Bring the sauce to a boil and cook, stirring, until it has thickened, about 5 minutes.

4. Heat the olive oil in a medium cast-iron pan over medium heat. Add the onion slices and remaining ¼ teaspoon salt and cook, stirring frequently, until they are a rich golden brown, about 25 minutes.

5. Preheat the oven to 350°F.

6. Spread ¼ cup of the chile sauce in the bottom of a 9 × 13-inch baking dish. Dip one tortilla at a time into the remaining sauce, then place it on a plate. Put about ½ cup of cooked onions, ¼ cup of queso fresco, and 1 tablespoon of olives in a line across the center of the tortilla. Roll the tortilla up tightly around the filling and place it in the baking dish, seam side down. Repeat this process until you've used up the remaining tortillas and onions.

7. Pour the remaining sauce over the enchiladas and sprinkle them with the remaining cheese and olives. Bake the enchiladas for about 40 minutes, until they are heated through and the cheese has just melted.

PORK RIBS STEAMED *in* APPLE CIDER

ACTIVE TIME
1 hour 10 minutes

TOTAL TIME
*2 hours 10 minutes, or
longer if resting overnight*

SERVES
8 to 10

Ribs are great for big crowds because they're super simple to cook, it's easy to make enough for a lot of people, and they're loved by both kids and adults. The thing that makes this recipe really great is that you steam the ribs in apple cider after they're grilled, which gives them a ton of sweet flavor and helps them become fall-off-the-bone tender. And because this last step doesn't take any hands-on work, you can grill all the meat ahead of time, then just set them to steam about 30 minutes before you plan to serve your meal, and they'll be hot and ready to go.

2 cups packed light brown sugar

¼ cup kosher salt

2 tablespoons sweet paprika

2 tablespoons garlic powder

2 teaspoons ground black pepper

2 teaspoons mustard powder

4 racks baby back pork ribs (about 12 pounds total), at room temperature

2 cups apple cider or apple juice

1. Mix together the brown sugar, salt, paprika, garlic powder, black pepper, and mustard powder in a medium bowl; set it aside.

2. Working with one rack at a time, place the ribs on a large cutting board, bone side up, and remove the silver skin by using a butter knife to loosen a corner of the membrane, then slowly pulling it off the meat.

3. Coat the ribs generously on both sides with the rub, pressing it into the meat, and transfer them to a sheet pan. Let the meat sit and absorb the rub for at least 20 minutes or (preferably) refrigerate it overnight, covered with plastic wrap, and bring to room temperature before cooking.

4. Heat a wood, charcoal, or gas grill to medium. (If you're working with charcoal or wood, pile your coals on one side of the grill and let the flames die down so you have hot, white coals; if you're using gas, the temperature should be around 350°F.) Grill the meat, bone side down, on the side of the grill farthest from the coals until the outside is golden with some dark charred spots and the crust has caramelized slightly, about 15 minutes. Flip the ribs and grill for another 15 minutes on the other side. Reduce the heat to low (or transfer the meat to a cooler part of the grill) and continue grilling for another 30 minutes, flipping occasionally so all sides get even heat.

5. Fit a large pot with a steamer and pour the cider into the bottom of the pot. Set the pot on the grill (or on the stove) and heat it until the liquid is steaming. Cut the ribs in half (or in thirds) so that they fit into the pot and put them in the steamer, making sure they don't touch the liquid. Cover the pot and steam the ribs slowly over low heat for 30 minutes.

GRILLED ANAHEIMS
with GARLIC SALT

ACTIVE TIME
45 minutes

TOTAL TIME
1 hour 40 minutes

SERVES
6 to 8

10 fresh Anaheim chiles

½ cup extra virgin olive oil

1 teaspoon garlic salt

I have been eating these grilled peppers at our family reunion every summer for as long as I can remember. I used to watch my great uncle, whom I called Tío, make them when I was a kid, and now our entire family often sits together before lunch grilling and peeling the peppers. We eat them with pretty much everything. They're great on steak or chicken, as a filling for quesadillas, on thick pieces of grilled garlic bread, or even with fresh tomatoes and creamy mozzarella. I can't get enough!

If you're not grilling, you can also prepare these peppers by setting them directly over the flame of a gas stove, or under a broiler.

---

1. Heat a wood, charcoal, or gas grill to high. (If you're working with charcoal or wood, you should have very hot, white coals and only a few final flames; if you're using gas, the temperature should be 350°F.)

2. Grill the peppers whole, turning them with tongs as the skin makes air bubbles and turns light brown. (The peppers may turn black, which is fine, but take them off the grill before the skin becomes ash.)

3. When the peppers look hot and bubbly, take them off the grill and immediately put them in a paper bag. Close the bag (folding the end over itself a couple of times) and let them cool and steam in their own moisture for about 20 minutes; this will loosen the skin so you can remove it more easily.

4. Remove one pepper from the bag, cut off the top (with the stem), and cut down one side so you can open the pepper up and lay it flat on a cutting board. Use the back of a knife to remove the pepper's skin, then turn it over and deseed it. Repeat with the remaining peppers.

5. Pull each pepper apart with your hands (as you would pull a piece of string cheese) into ½-inch-wide strips.

6. Mix the pepper strips with the olive oil and garlic salt in a large bowl. Let the peppers marinate for at least 15 minutes, then serve at room temperature.

CHILE RELLENO CASSEROLE

ACTIVE TIME
20 minutes

TOTAL TIME
1 hour 25 minutes

SERVES
6 to 8

Unsalted butter, at room temperature, for greasing

One 14.5-ounce can diced tomatoes, with their liquid

6 poblano chiles, grilled, skinned, and pulled into strips (see page 133) or one 28-ounce can fire-roasted green chiles, drained

1 pound freshly grated Monterey Jack

12 large eggs

½ cup heavy cream

½ teaspoon kosher salt

⅛ teaspoon ground black pepper

I love classic chiles rellenos—I make them a lot in the summer, when poblanos are in season—but the traditional method of dipping them in batter and frying just a couple at a time makes them hard to cook for a crowd. This casserole solves that problem. It has all the fresh flavors I love, but I can make it ahead of time and then put it in the oven just before my guests show up. It even makes a great brunch dish; just assemble it the day before and throw it in the fridge overnight so it's ready to bake the next morning.

1. Preheat the oven to 350°F. Grease a 9 × 13-inch baking or casserole dish with the butter.

2. Spoon one-fourth of the tomatoes (and their liquid) into the dish (just enough to moisten the bottom of the pan) and spread them out evenly. Spread one-fourth of the chile strips evenly across the tomatoes, then scatter one-fourth of the cheese evenly over the vegetables. The ingredients will have lots of space in between them. Repeat this layering process three more times with the remaining ingredients to make 4 layers, reserving the last quarter of the cheese.

3. Whisk the eggs and cream with the salt and pepper in a medium bowl. Slowly pour the egg mixture over the casserole, adding it evenly to all parts of the dish. Let the casserole sit for 5 minutes so that the egg soaks in (you can use a fork to push the ingredients down into the egg if something looks dry). Sprinkle on the reserved cheese.

4. Bake the casserole for 40 to 45 minutes, until it looks puffy and has a golden top. Let it rest for 15 minutes to firm up, then cut into squares and serve warm.

TOMATO SALAD *with* CORN AND KALAMATA OLIVES

ACTIVE TIME
10 minutes

TOTAL TIME
10 minutes

SERVES
6 to 8

FOR THE SALAD

5 medium-large heirloom tomatoes

1 cup mixed cherry tomatoes

12 kalamata olives

1 large ear corn

Freshly grated Parmesan (optional)

Small handful basil sprigs (with flowers attached, if you have them)

FOR THE CHAMPAGNE VINAIGRETTE

½ cup extra virgin olive oil

¼ cup champagne vinegar (or red wine vinegar)

2 teaspoons honey

1 teaspoon kosher salt

1 teaspoon Dijon mustard

¼ teaspoon ground black pepper

My friend Katie and I plant lots of different kinds of vegetables every year, and we always make sure to plant lots and lots of tomatoes. The best ones are ready in September and October, when the last of the year's really hot days have made them sweet. In this bright salad, I combine them with fresh corn, which adds a sweet note to balance the tomatoes' acidity, and kalamata olives for their great salty flavor. The result is pure deliciousness. I also like to add Parmesan, because I just love cheese on everything.

MAKE THE SALAD

1. Cut 3 of the heirloom tomatoes into ½-inch-thick slices and lay them on a large platter. Cut the remaining 2 heirloom tomatoes into large wedges and arrange them on top of the slices.

2. Cut half of the cherry tomatoes and some of the kalamata olives in half and scatter both the cut and the uncut tomatoes and olives on top of the larger tomatoes.

3. Cut the kernels off the corn ear and sprinkle them on top of the tomatoes, letting them fall between the slices.

DRESS THE SALAD

1. Combine the olive oil, vinegar, honey, salt, mustard, and pepper in a jar and seal it tightly. Shake the jar until the dressing is fully emulsified.

2. Drizzle the dressing over the tomatoes, corn, and olives. Scatter the Parmesan, if using, generously over the top of the salad and tuck basil leaves—individual leaves, small sprigs, and some flowering sprigs, if you have them—into the salad in whatever way looks best.

SPANISH RICE

ACTIVE TIME
5 minutes

TOTAL TIME
35 minutes

SERVES
4

2 large Roma tomatoes, cored and quartered

½ yellow onion, cut into 4 pieces

2 garlic cloves

2 tablespoons extra virgin olive oil

1 cup long-grain white rice

2 cups Turkey or Chicken Broth (page 210) or store-bought

1 teaspoon kosher salt

This is one of my all-time favorite rice recipes. I make it for my family all the time, especially when we have fresh Roma tomatoes from the garden. We eat it with tacos and chiles rellenos, and it even goes great with steak. I also like to make a large pot of it when I'm having a barbecue.

1. Put the tomatoes, onion, and garlic in a blender or food processor and puree until the mixture has the consistency of a smoothie. Set it aside.

2. Heat the olive oil in a medium saucepan over medium heat. Add the rice and sauté it for 1 minute.

3. Pour the tomato mixture into the saucepan, add the broth and salt, and mix well.

4. Bring the mixture to a boil, then cover the pot, turn the heat to low, and cook the rice over medium heat for 20 minutes. Turn off the heat and let the pot sit, covered, for 5 minutes.

5. Use a wooden spoon to fluff and mix the rice.

RED WINE SANGRIA

ACTIVE TIME
15 minutes

TOTAL TIME
*2 hours 15 minutes,
including resting (or
longer if refrigerating
overnight)*

SERVES
6

2 oranges

1 cup brandy

½ cup freshly squeezed
orange juice or lemon juice

½ bottle red wine

2 cups Homemade Simple
Syrup (page 277)

1 cinnamon stick (optional,
for a richer flavor)

1 lemon

1 pear

Ice cubes

Sparkling water (optional)

I fell in love with sangria when I was studying in Spain. Sure, it's a bit touristy—in Spain, it often just comes from a box—but I love it! It's a really festive way to start a meal. And because it's served on ice, it's bright and refreshing, even though it's made with red wine. I often mix up a batch for parties—my family made huge vats of sangria for my wedding—and these days I like to use it as a welcome drink to serve to guests at our Ranch Table events. For this version, I also took inspiration from the drink that most Spaniards actually prefer, tinto de verano (wine mixed with a citrusy soda), and added a bit of sparkling water to make the drink even fresher. I've used very classic fruits here, but you can add any fruit you like. You should use an affordable wine but something good enough to drink on its own.

1. Cut the peel off one of the oranges: First, cut the stem end and bottom off, making sure to remove the peel and the white pith but not too much of the flesh. Set the orange down on a cut end and cut the peel and pith off in strips, going from top to bottom and working your way around the orange. Cut the peeled orange into large pieces.

2. Put the orange pieces into a 10-cup pitcher (or a similar container) with the brandy and let it soak for 1 hour or (preferably) refrigerate it overnight.

3. Add the orange juice, wine, simple syrup, and cinnamon stick (if using) to the pitcher and fill it with ice, then refrigerate for 1 hour.

4. Slice the other (unpeeled) orange crosswise into rounds. Cut the lemon crosswise into rounds and quarter the pear. Add the fruit to the pitcher.

5. To serve, fill a glass with ice, add ½ cup of the sangria (plus some of the fruit), then top it off with ¼ cup of sparkling water, if using.

TIP: The level of sweetness in this sangria will depend on the flavors of your fruit and your wine. If you're worried that it will be too sweet, add the simple syrup a little at a time and taste as you go.

BLACKBERRY MARGARITA

ACTIVE TIME
2 minutes

TOTAL TIME
2 minutes

MAKES
1 cocktail

Kosher salt, for the rim

¼ lime, for the rim

Ice cubes

1½ ounces Blackberry Simple Syrup (recipe follows)

1 tablespoon freshly squeezed lime juice

2 ounces silver tequila

2 ounces club soda (optional)

I've always loved picking the wild blackberries that grow on the fences around the big vegetable garden behind the Casa. When the plants are especially full of fruit, I bring some back to the house to make margaritas; the fruit nicely balances the tartness of the limes. The blackberry simple syrup that flavors the drinks is also great in sparkling water.

1. Pour ¼ cup of salt onto a small plate. Rub the lime quarter along the rim of a large, short glass, then dip the rim in the salt to coat it.

2. Fill the glass with ice. Pour the blackberry simple syrup and lime juice into the glass, add the tequila, and top the drink off with the club soda, if using. Stir before serving.

VARIATION: PITCHER MARGARITAS

To make a pitcher of drinks, combine 2 cups of silver tequila, 1 cup of lime juice, and 1½ cups of blackberry simple syrup in a pitcher. To serve, fill a cup with ice, add enough drink mix to fill two-thirds of the cup, then top with club soda (if using).

BLACKBERRY SIMPLE SYRUP

1 cup blackberries

1 cup granulated sugar

1 cup water

ACTIVE TIME
5 minutes

TOTAL TIME
35 minutes

MAKES
about 1½ cups

1. Combine the blackberries, sugar, and water in a small saucepan and bring the mixture to a boil over high heat, stirring occasionally.

2. Reduce the heat to medium-low and simmer until the berries have lost some of their color and have softened, about 10 minutes. Remove the syrup from the heat and mash the berries against the side of the pot with a spoon.

3. Let the syrup cool to room temperature, about 20 minutes, then strain it through a fine-mesh sieve to remove the seeds and berry skins.

BEACH COOKOUT

MELON WITH LIME AND CHILE · 151

GRILLED FISH AND JALAPEÑO TACOS · 153

GRILLED SUMMER SQUASH · 155
with Pesto Dressing 156

STRAWBERRY CHOCOLATE CHIP ICE CREAM SANDWICHES · 159
with Homemade Strawberry Chocolate Chip Ice Cream 160
and Chewy Chocolate Chip Cookies 161

BY THE END OF SUMMER, THE CENTRAL COAST IS PARCHED
and dry. We have not had rain for five months, and the golden grasses covering the hills are bleached in the sun until they are a faint whitish beige. Dust from the roads rises with every footstep and passing truck. By breakfast, I can feel the heat creeping into the house, and by lunch, all the animals have congregated in the shady spots below the trees or along the creek's banks.

When we know the weather is going to be especially hot, Austin and I will sometimes cut out early and take the kids to the coast so we can all play in the ocean and cool down. Ranch work doesn't stick to a Monday through Friday schedule, so we rest when we can, and if we've had a busy weekend, we take a break midweek when the beaches are less crowded. It's hard to relax on the ranch—there's always something that needs to be done—so getting away is important for everyone.

Today is going to be a scorcher, so we're up and out early, feeding animals and checking cows before the sun even peeks over the hills. When we're done watering the animals, we'll head to a nearby beach for a nice long day of fun.

Instead of packing sandwiches, I decide I'll make something a little more festive when we get there. The beach we're going to has camping spots and allows cooking, and we have a portable mini fire pit designed for grilling that I can easily fit in the back of the truck. I load our big cooler with dry ice and things that I can prep and cook outdoors: I grab some frozen fish that Austin caught a few weeks ago to make tacos and a jar of fresh pico de gallo that I made yesterday. I pack up some of the summer squash, which has been exploding in the ranch garden this month and is great grilled, and make a really quick pesto to dress it with. A melon from the garden and some limes and spices go into a shopping bag. Last, I grab some treats from the deep freezer—ice cream sandwiches that I made with homemade chocolate chip cookies and strawberry chocolate chip ice cream—and put them in the cooler too.

We pile into our truck and head toward the coast, and in just fifteen minutes we're at the beach.

ψ

While the ranch can feel very landlocked sometimes, the ocean is a really important part of our lives. I spent big parts of my childhood playing in the sand and swimming in the waves, and when I was a teenager, the beaches up and down the coast were great places to meet up with friends. The water here is fairly warm in the summer, and the waves are great all year round. The Santa Barbara coast is also full of marine life, and the waters provide an abundance of seafood. Local fishermen and divers bring in everything from halibut and white seabass to spot prawns and urchin.

Austin loves to fish and often goes out with family and friends to catch white sea bass, halibut, or rockfish. On these mornings, Austin leaves the house at three so that they can get to the harbor in Santa Barbara before daylight, when the water is calm. By late afternoon, he's back with fresh, cleaned fish that we can cook up right away or freeze for later.

ψ

The beach we picked today is one of our favorites, a quintessential California strip of sand lined with palm trees on a relatively small cove. The temperature is noticeably cooler here than it is at home. We find a nice spot on the beach to set up the grill and a makeshift wooden table to serve as a base camp. Austin helps me start the fire, then sets up a chair to watch the kids while they swim. We're not surfers, but like lots of California kids, my boys are interested, and they see tackling waves on the longboards we got them last year as a challenge. This spot has a nice break some days and often attracts surfers, but right now it's pretty calm, and perfect for beginners. Later, Jack and Hank will probably take their fishing rods and tackle boxes and head out to the rock point, at the edge of the cove, to see if they can catch anything. We also have a couple of shovels—not beach toys but big metal shovels that we use on the ranch—that they can use to build forts in the sand.

I'm excited about the food, so I get out a big cutting board and cut up the melon for the boys to come grab when they get hungry. Each slice gets a squeeze of lime juice and a dusting of my sugar-chile powder, which work together to bring out the fruit's rich flavors. When the small fire is ready, I cut the squash in half and put them on to cook with a bit of oil, salt, and pepper.

While the squash is grilling, I prep the fish. Instead of cooking it directly on the grill, where it will dry out and might stick, I opt to put the fillets in foil with some butter and garlic, then add lemon and green onions to some and lime and sliced jalapeños to others. I fold the foil into little envelope-like packets around the fish, and when I put them on the grill, the fillets cook gently in the fat while the citrus and other ingredients infuse everything with a subtle flavor. I also toast some tortillas on the grill to give them a little bit of char.

As I'm cooking, the boys see some friends walking past, and I take a minute to say hello and invite everyone to come have a taco later. This beach is popular with local families, and we almost always run into friends here, especially in the summer when the kids are out of school. In an area full of ranches, farms, and vineyards, we might not have neighbors just across the street, but we're never lacking in community. We still have lots of places where people congregate—like this beach, or the main streets of the small local towns that dot this part of the county—and the whole area has a great small-town vibe.

By noon, lunch is ready, and the boys and Austin are salty and sandy and very hungry from all the swimming. The kids crowd around as I portion the fish and salsa into the tortillas and watch them wolf down the vegetables and what's left of the fruit. It's a perfect seaside meal—light but filling and full of summery flavors. It's nice to sit together for the meal, but the calm only lasts for a moment before they run back to a lean-to fort they've started building from dried palm fronds.

Austin and I clean up and put out the fire, then we drag the cooler onto the beach so that we can have the ice cream sandwiches when the kids inevitably get hungry again in a couple of hours. With the cooking done, I grab my stand-up paddleboard and head out into the cool, bracing water.

MELON *with* LIME AND CHILE

ACTIVE TIME
5 minutes

TOTAL TIME
5 minutes

SERVES
4 to 6

1 teaspoon granulated
sugar

1 teaspoon kosher salt

¼ teaspoon chili powder

One 3½-pound cantaloupe

1 tablespoon freshly
squeezed lime juice

Sometimes when we need a quick snack, I throw together an easy, homemade version of the seasoned cut fruit you can pick up from Mexican American fruit stands all over California. I make my own super-simple salt and spice mix so that I can control the amount of spice (to keep it kid-friendly). The result is just slightly sweet, sour, salty, smoky, and spicy and brings out the aromas and flavors of the melon instead of taking over.

1. Mix the sugar, salt, and chili powder in a small bowl.

2. Cut the cantaloupe in half and remove the seeds. Cut the cantaloupe into wedges (about 1 inch thick at the rind), and then cut the flesh away from the rind but leave it in place so the rind acts as a kind of plate.

3. Place the cantaloupe slices on a serving plate, rind side down, and cut the flesh into large pieces, leaving them sitting on the rind. Drizzle the lime juice over the pieces and sprinkle them with the spice mixture.

GRILLED FISH *and* JALAPENO TACOS

ACTIVE TIME
40 minutes

TOTAL TIME
50 minutes

MAKES
8 tacos

1 pound boneless white fish fillets (rockfish, lingcod, cabezon, or any kind of cod will work), divided into 4 portions

12 thick fresh lime slices (from about 3 limes)

4 tablespoons unsalted butter

1 teaspoon kosher salt

Ground black pepper

1 teaspoon smoked paprika

8 cilantro sprigs

8 large garlic cloves, cut in half

3 jalapeños, stemmed and cut into thick slices

Eight 8-inch corn tortillas

Pico de Gallo (page 21) or store-bought

Cooking fish on a grill can be a great, quick way to make dinner, but it can also be a bit tricky, since fish is a lot more delicate than other meat and can break apart, stick to the grill, or fall through onto the fire. My favorite fix is to grill the fish in foil packets instead of putting it directly over the flame. Foil keeps the fish from drying out and lets me flavor the fillets with whatever ingredients I want. For these tacos, I add a bit of butter, which melts and sort of steams the fish, and some garlic, jalapeños, and sliced limes.

1. Heat a wood or charcoal grill to high or a gas grill to medium-high. (If you're working with charcoal or wood, you should have very hot, white coals and only a few final flames; if you're using gas, the temperature should be 350°F.)

2. While the grill is heating, prepare 4 large pieces of heavy-duty foil (or 8 sheets of regular foil, doubled up). Divide the fillets among the foil sheets and top each with one-quarter of the ingredients: 3 lime slices, 1 tablespoon butter (cut into small pieces), ¼ teaspoon salt, some pepper, ¼ teaspoon paprika, 2 cilantro sprigs, 2 garlic cloves (4 halves), and one-quarter of the jalapeño slices.

3. Fold the long sides of the foil up to the top, above the fish, and pinch them together, folding the edges over just a bit. Pinch down the sides of the foil, folding them over a bit as well, so that the foil is totally sealed; this will give you packets with a large pocket of air above the fish fillets, so they can steam in the moisture from the butter.

4. When the grill is hot, place the packets on the grill and cook until the fish is opaque and tender, about 25 minutes. (To check, carefully open the top of a packet, making sure not to let anything spill out, and poke the fish with a fork; it should flake easily under the tines.)

5. When the fish has cooked, put the tortillas on the grill and toast them lightly, flipping them with tongs a couple of times to make sure they're not burning, for about 1 minute.

6. Open the packets of fish, break the fillets into large pieces, and divide the meat among the tortillas. Add any of the flavorings you like (except the lime slices) and serve with the pico.

GRILLED SUMMER SQUASH

ACTIVE TIME
25 minutes

TOTAL TIME
40 minutes

SERVES
4 to 6

3 medium zucchini or
yellow summer squash
(1 pound)

½ cup extra virgin olive oil

1 tablespoon kosher salt

¼ teaspoon ground black
pepper

¼ teaspoon garlic powder

Pesto Dressing (recipe
follows)

Nasturtium flowers
(optional)

I could eat this dish every day.

If you've ever grown zucchini or summer squash, you know that, at some point in the summer, there's always too much squash in your kitchen. When that happens, I throw it on the grill and serve it with a quick pesto dressing that I make with a little bit of red wine vinegar. I also like to top everything with some peppery nasturtium flowers. The combination of flavors screams summer, and I never get tired of it.

While putting flowers on grilled vegetables might seem a little bit extra, they're a natural part of my summer garden and I love adding them to everything. I always plant flowers in my vegetable gardens, not only because they're good for bringing pollinators but also because pests might eat the flowers before they get to my vegetable plants.

1. Heat a wood or charcoal grill to high or gas grill to medium-high. (If working with charcoal or wood, you should have very hot, white coals and only a few final flames; if you're using gas, the temperature should be 350°F.)

2. Trim both ends of the squash, then cut each one in half lengthwise. Lay the squash on a baking pan, cut sides up, and drizzle ¼ cup of the olive oil onto the squash. Using a pastry brush, spread the oil on the squash to coat it. Flip the squash, so they're sitting cut sides down, and use the brush to spread the remaining ¼ cup olive oil onto the back sides. Flip the squash cut side up.

3. Mix the salt, pepper, and garlic powder in a small bowl. Sprinkle half the mixture over the cut sides of the squash; reserve the remaining mixture.

4. Place the squash on the grill, cut sides down. Sprinkle the rest of the salt mixture on the skin of the squash. Grill the squash until the cut sides have nice dark-brown char marks, about 10 minutes. Flip the squash over and cook them until the bottoms have a nice char and the squash have become softened and slightly limp, another 10 minutes or so.

5. Transfer the squash to a serving plate. Shake the jar of dressing to mix well, then spoon about ½ cup over the squash. Top with the flowers, if using.

TIP: For this dish, you'll want to use medium squash that are still firm in the center; the bigger ones get too soft and full of seeds.

PESTO DRESSING

2 cups loosely packed basil leaves

¾ cup freshly grated Parmesan

¼ cup pine nuts

1 tablespoon freshly squeezed lemon juice

1 teaspoon kosher salt

2 garlic cloves

¾ cup extra virgin olive oil

2 tablespoons red wine vinegar

ACTIVE TIME
5 minutes

TOTAL TIME
5 minutes

MAKES
1½ cups

Put the basil, Parmesan, pine nuts, lemon juice, salt, and garlic in a food processor and pulse until the basil is shredded into small pieces. Scrape the sides of the food processor, then continue to pulse, drizzling in the olive oil as you do. Scrape the sides again, then add the vinegar. Pulse until everything is well mixed. (If you want to use this pesto on pasta, leave out the vinegar.)

STRAWBERRY CHOCOLATE CHIP ICE CREAM SANDWICHES

ACTIVE TIME
15 minutes

TOTAL TIME
2 hours 15 minutes

MAKES
12 ice cream sandwiches

3 cups Homemade Strawberry Chocolate Chip Ice Cream (page 160) or store-bought ice cream

24 Chewy Chocolate Chip Cookies (page 161)

I really love chocolate, so I love these sandwiches, which have chopped chocolate in both the ice cream and the cookies. That said, you could totally make these sandwiches with good store-bought strawberry ice cream, and they'd still be so good!

1. Place a sheet pan in the freezer.

2. Scoop about ¼ cup of ice cream onto the bottom side of a cookie. Top the scoop with a second cookie of about the same size, then very gently press them together. (You'll have about 1 inch of ice cream between the cookies.) Immediately place the sandwich on the sheet in the freezer.

3. Repeat to make 12 ice cream sandwiches.

4. Freeze the sandwiches until the ice cream is very solid, at least 2 hours. To store or transport the sandwiches, wrap each one in some parchment paper and then in an outer layer of foil, and store them in a freezer or on dry ice.

HOMEMADE STRAWBERRY CHOCOLATE CHIP ICE CREAM

ACTIVE TIME
15 minutes

TOTAL TIME
6 hours, including chilling (or longer if chilling overnight)

MAKES
6 cups

1 cup heavy cream

1 cup whole milk

½ teaspoon pure vanilla extract

¼ teaspoon kosher salt

¾ cup granulated sugar

6 egg yolks

1 pound strawberries (fresh or frozen)

4 ounces semisweet chocolate, cut into small pieces

SPECIAL TOOLS

Ice cream maker

I've had an ice cream maker for years, and I love experimenting with new flavors. Once you get comfortable with a basic vanilla ice cream recipe, you can then add all kinds of fruit purees, nuts—or even coffee! (Yes, please!) Here, I've combined two classic ice cream flavors— strawberry and chocolate chip—into one.

Check the instructions on your ice cream maker; some machines require you to freeze the tub for a full 24 hours before you begin.

---

1. Combine the cream, milk, vanilla, and salt in a medium saucepan and heat the mixture over medium heat until it starts to steam; take care not to let it scald or boil.

2. In the meantime, put ½ cup of the sugar and the egg yolks in a stand mixer fitted with the whisk attachment and whisk on medium speed until the mixture forms ribbons, about 2 minutes. Alternatively, whisk them by hand in a medium bowl.

3. Remove the cream mixture from the heat. With the mixer still on medium speed, slowly add half the hot cream mixture into the yolks, pouring it in a thin stream (to temper the eggs). (If you whisked by hand, whisk in the thin stream.)

4. Transfer the egg mixture to the pot with the remaining cream mixture and cook over low heat, whisking constantly, for 2 minutes. Remove the pot from the heat.

5. Combine the strawberries and the remaining ¼ cup sugar in a blender or food processor and puree until smooth.

6. Pour the warm custard mixture into a heatproof container. Add the strawberry puree and whisk everything together. Let the mixture come to room temperature, then refrigerate it until very cold, at least 4 hours or (preferably) overnight. (If using frozen berries, skip this step.)

7. Pour the custard mixture into the ice cream maker, stir in the chocolate, and process the ice cream according to the manufacturer's instructions.

8. When the ice cream has set (but is still relatively soft), cover it with plastic wrap (or transfer it to pint containers) and freeze it until it's fairly solid.

CHEWY CHOCOLATE CHIP COOKIES

ACTIVE TIME
10 minutes

TOTAL TIME
35 minutes

MAKES
18 to 20 cookies

1 cup extra virgin olive oil

1 cup lightly packed light brown sugar

½ cup granulated sugar

2 large eggs

1 teaspoon pure vanilla extract

2½ cups all-purpose flour

1 teaspoon kosher salt

1 teaspoon baking soda

8 ounces semisweet or bittersweet chocolate, finely chopped

This is a classic chocolate chip cookie with a nice chewy center and lots of chocolate. The cookies are big enough to use for ice cream sandwiches (page 159), but they're also perfect on their own. Their chewy texture is designed to soak up a bit of liquid, whether that's melting ice cream or just cold milk. I use olive oil instead of butter in these cookies; it keeps them from getting too hard when I freeze them for ice cream sandwiches and adds a slightly more yummy flavor (though you don't actually taste the oil).

1. Preheat the oven to 350°F. Line two sheet pans with parchment paper.

2. Put the olive oil and both sugars into the bowl of a stand mixer fitted with the paddle attachment or a large bowl (if using a hand mixer) and beat them together on medium speed until light and fluffy, about 2 minutes.

3. Add the eggs and vanilla to the oil-sugar mixture and beat on medium speed until combined. Stop the mixer, scrape the sides and bottom of the bowl with a spoon or rubber spatula, and beat again until everything is combined.

4. Mix the flour, salt, and baking soda together in a medium bowl. Add half of this mixture to the mixer and beat on low until just combined. Add the remaining flour mixture and beat everything on low until combined, then scrape the sides and bottom of the bowl again to make sure everything is fully incorporated.

5. Add the chopped chocolate to the bowl and use a wooden spoon to mix it into the dough.

6. Portion out 3 tablespoons of the dough, roll it gently into a ball in your hands, then press it down onto one of the sheet pans, flattening it slightly. Repeat, leaving plenty of space between each cookie; you should be able to fit 6 cookies on each sheet.

7. Bake the cookies for 12 minutes, until puffy in the center and lightly browned on the edges. Let them cool on the pan for 10 minutes before transferring them to a cooling rack.

8. Repeat to use the remaining dough. Store the cookies in an airtight container for 2 to 3 days or freeze for up to 2 weeks.

PART THREE

FALL

Back to School Dinner
Garden Harvest Feast
Cider Press Potluck

BACK TO SCHOOL DINNER

WEEKNIGHT STEAKS WITH SWEET ONIONS · 171

with Blue Cheese Sauce 172

GREEN BEANS WITH HERB SALT · 175

with Balsamic Glaze 175

BOILED BABY POTATOES WITH BUTTER AND PARSLEY · 176

**PEANUT BUTTER MERINGUE PIE
WITH A CHOCOLATE GRAHAM CRACKER CRUST · 177**

THERE'S ALWAYS A LOT OF EXCITEMENT IN THE AIR AT THE
beginning of the school year. During the summer, the boys spend many of their days with Austin and me, coming along to fix fences or water lines. They also spend time on their own, building forts, hiking around the ranch, and playing in the creeks. So the start of the school year, and the return to a steady schedule, is a big shift for all of us.

By early September, the kids' days are completely taken up by school, soccer, playdates, and all kinds of after-school activities. Mornings are busy—we have a long drive to school, and we have to load up all our bags, lunches, and gear for the day—and Austin is also up and out early to get a jumpstart on projects. So during those first weeks, when we're just getting back into our regular routines, I give family dinners a little extra attention. We use the time to eat a good meal together and catch up on the day.

For weeknight meals, I focus on making simple, hearty foods. My kids come home really hungry, and I want to make sure I'm serving plenty of the essentials: protein, starch, and vegetables. I also stick to foods that come together quickly, so I can spend my time sitting at the table instead of standing over the stove. One of my regular, go-to dinners on nights like these is a couple of easy steaks that I cook quickly, like New York strips, skirt steaks, or flatiron steaks. They're always a hit with everyone, and while I panfry them, I can put some small potatoes on to simmer. When the meat is cooked and resting, I quickly boil some green beans and flavor them with a bit of herbed salt and balsamic glaze. The entire meal is on the table in less than forty minutes from start to finish, and everything can be served right out of the pan it's made in.

Austin has to run some errands in town, so he picks up the kids at the end of the day, and I wrap up my work and start cooking while they're on their way home. I always love quiet time in the kitchen and enjoy these few minutes of calm. The kids come in full of energy and eager to tell us about the day, and in just a few minutes, we're all sitting around the table. We talk about their classes and teachers and hear about the new friends they're making and the old friends they're reconnecting with after the summer. The food disappears fast, in big bites, between stories about soccer goals and science experiments.

At this time of year, the evening doesn't end when the last of the dishes are scraped. Since the weather is still warm in September, and it stays light until bedtime, we often take advantage of this extra sunlight to get the kids back outside and let them run around before we all settle in for homework and bedtime. On many evenings, we drive to the hills at the back of the ranch to fly kites. I absolutely love kites; my parents always had them around when I was a kid, and there's something about the simple fun of getting them airborne and watching them sail around that brings a smile at any age.

Tonight, I also pack an after-dinner treat: a peanut butter pie in a chocolate crust, topped with toasted meringue. My mom has been making these pies for Thanksgiving for years, and over time

I've taken her recipe and adapted it, adding a little more chocolate (of course!) and a bit more peanut butter. I now also make this pie for summer barbecues, but it's one of those pies that can be made and enjoyed all year long.

There's always a good wind on the hills at the Rosa, the piece of land at the back of the ranch. *Rosa* means "pink" in Spanish, but no one really knows how this spot got its name. If you stand at the top of the ridge, you can see the Santa Ynez Valley to the east and the ocean and the Channel Islands to the west. Sunsets up here are some of the most beautiful I've seen, and in the evening there's a wonderful breeze coming in from the Pacific.

When we get up to the highest part of the ranch, we stop the truck and pile out. Before I know it, the kids' kites are so far up in the air that I have to crane my neck to see them dancing against the blue sky. We walk down the hills a bit, letting out string as we go, and the boys try to get their kites as high as they possibly can.

When the sun hits the horizon in the distance, and the light is about to start its long, slow fade, I call everyone back to the truck. No one wants to put away the kites, but as soon as I yell "Pie!" they come running. We all sit on the back of the truck together, and I dole out big slices. As we eat, the sun starts to sink into the ocean, and the entire sky turns a vivid, hot pink. It might just be the most stunning California sunset I've ever seen, and as I watch it fade, I wonder, probably for the hundredth time, if this sunset view is how the Rosa got its name.

WEEKNIGHT STEAKS
with SWEET ONIONS

ACTIVE TIME
15 minutes

TOTAL TIME
15 minutes

SERVES
4

1¼ teaspoons kosher salt, plus more to taste

¼ teaspoon ground black pepper

Two 1-inch-thick New York strip steaks (¾ to 1 pound each), at room temperature

2 sweet onions, such as Vidalia or Walla Walla

3 tablespoons extra virgin olive oil

3 tablespoons unsalted butter

1 garlic clove, smashed

2 bay leaves

Blue Cheese Sauce (optional; recipe follows)

When I was a kid, my dad's go-to dinner was steak. On nights when he cooked, he would make us a simple meal of steak, peas, and rice, then my brother and I would sit on a blanket and watch an old movie while we ate. It always felt like a really special night, and my dad was great at making cold, dark evenings something to look forward to.

Steak is one of the easiest, quickest meals you can make. You really don't need many ingredients at all if you have good meat—just some salt and pepper and maybe a little butter to baste with. Sometimes I make an easy sauce for the adults, like a blue cheese sauce, which I love (see below), but you don't really need it. My dad usually just added some Worcestershire sauce or A1—which was the popular thing to use in the 1980s.

1. Rub 1 teaspoon of the salt and all the pepper into the steaks and let them rest for 30 minutes.

2. While the steaks are resting, cut the onions into ¼-inch-thick rounds. Put the onions, 2 tablespoons of the olive oil, and the remaining ¼ teaspoon salt into a large cast-iron pan. Cook over medium heat, stirring occasionally, until the onions are soft and golden brown, about 10 minutes, then remove them from the pan; set them aside.

3. Add the remaining 1 tablespoon olive oil to the pan and heat it over medium heat until the oil smokes just a bit, about 1 minute. Add the steaks and sear them for 30 seconds on each side.

4. Add the butter, garlic, and bay leaves to the pan. Once the butter melts, tilt the pan so the butter, garlic, and bay leaves pool to one side. While one hand is tilting the pan slightly, use the other to spoon the butter over the steaks, basting them, for 2 minutes, then flip the steaks over and baste them again for another 1 to 2 minutes, until they reach an internal temperature of 125° to 130°F for rare, 145°F for medium, or your preferred doneness.

5. Pull the pan off the heat, remove the bay leaves, and return the onions to the pan. Taste the pan sauce and adjust the seasoning.

6. Serve with the Blue Cheese Sauce, if using.

BLUE CHEESE SAUCE

¼ cup heavy cream

2 tablespoons unsalted
butter

½ cup crumbled
Gorgonzola or other blue
cheese

1 teaspoon Worcestershire
sauce

¼ teaspoon kosher salt
Serve warm.

ACTIVE TIME
5 minutes

TOTAL TIME
5 minutes

MAKES
½ cup

Combine the cream and butter in a medium saucepan and cook them over low heat until the butter melts, about 3 minutes. Add the cheese, Worcestershire sauce, and salt and whisk slowly until the cheese has melted, about 2 minutes. Serve warm.

GREEN BEANS *with* HERB SALT

ACTIVE TIME
10 minutes

TOTAL TIME
30 minutes

SERVES
4, with extra herb salt

1 tablespoon plus
1 teaspoon kosher salt

½ teaspoon dried oregano

¼ teaspoon dried
marjoram

⅛ teaspoon ground black
pepper

1 pound green beans,
trimmed

1 tablespoon extra virgin
olive oil

Balsamic Glaze (recipe
follows) or store-bought

We grow a lot of green beans in the garden because they're an easy, bright vegetable to add to any family meal. Sometimes I make them with just a bit of oil and salt, and other times I take a few extra minutes to make an herb salt to sprinkle on them. For this version, I also added an easy balsamic glaze.

1. Mix 1 tablespoon of the salt with the oregano, marjoram, and pepper in a small bowl; set aside.

2. Bring a large pot of water to a boil and add the remaining 1 teaspoon salt. Add the green beans to the pot and cook them until their color brightens but they are still slightly crunchy, 2 to 3 minutes. Drain the beans and transfer them to a serving plate.

3. Pour the olive oil over the beans and mix them to coat. Sprinkle ¾ teaspoon of the herb salt onto the beans and mix to coat. Drizzle with some of the balsamic glaze.

TIP: If you want to keep your beans bright and green, dunk them in ice water when they come out of the boiling water.

BALSAMIC GLAZE

½ cup balsamic vinegar

3 tablespoons dark brown
sugar

ACTIVE TIME
10 minutes

TOTAL TIME
25 minutes

MAKES
½ cup

Combine the vinegar and brown sugar in a small saucepan and bring the mixture to a boil over medium heat, stirring to dissolve the sugar crystals. Reduce the heat to low and simmer until the liquid has reduced to a thick glaze, about 5 minutes. Transfer the glaze to a jar and let it cool for about 15 minutes before using.

BOILED BABY POTATOES
with BUTTER AND PARSLEY

ACTIVE TIME
5 minutes

TOTAL TIME
35 minutes

SERVES
4

12 to 15 baby red potatoes
(1 pound)

½ teaspoon kosher salt

3 tablespoons unsalted
butter

1 cup flat-leaf parsley,
roughly chopped

One afternoon when the boys were very young, I went to my parents' house feeling exhausted, and my mom asked me to stay for dinner. She cooked a super-simple meal, including these potatoes, and we sat in her cozy dining room, where she let Jack light the candles on the table. I felt so cared for and so grateful. This dish could not be any easier, but it holds a special place in my heart now because whenever I make it, I'm reminded of how lucky I am to be able to raise my kids just up the road from my parents.

1. Put the potatoes in a medium saucepan and cover them with water. Bring the water to a boil over high heat, then add ¼ teaspoon of the salt.

2. Boil the potatoes until fork-tender, about 15 minutes.

3. Drain the potatoes, then put them back into the hot saucepan. Add the butter to the pan, then cover the pan with a lid until the butter has mostly melted, about 2 minutes.

4. Add the parsley and the remaining ¼ teaspoon salt to the potatoes and use a large spoon to mix well.

PEANUT BUTTER MERINGUE PIE *with* A CHOCOLATE GRAHAM CRACKER CRUST

ACTIVE TIME
1 hour

TOTAL TIME
4 hours 25 minutes,
including chilling
(or longer if it chills
overnight)

SERVES
6 to 8

FOR THE CRUST

3 cups crumbs from
chocolate (or regular)
graham crackers

6 tablespoons (¾ stick)
unsalted butter, melted

¼ teaspoon kosher salt

2 ounces semisweet
chocolate, finely chopped

FOR THE CRUMBLE

1 cup powdered sugar,
sifted

¾ cup creamy salted
peanut butter

½ teaspoon ground
cinnamon

Peanut butter pie is a family favorite. We make it every Thanksgiving and for other celebrations and dinners. Most versions call for mixing peanut butter with cream cheese, but this one is more of a custard with a couple of layers of peanut butter crumble. The result is a really creamy, tender pie. I adapted this filling from an old community cookbook that my mom used to use; my version is a little richer and has more peanut butter. Most important, mine has a chocolate crust (made from chocolate graham crackers crushed in a food processor) with a layer of chocolate over it. Then the whole thing is topped with a fluffy meringue.

Custard takes as long as it takes to firm up when you're whisking it in a double boiler. The timing will depend on everything from the size of your bowl to how much water you have in the pot, and there's not much you can do to move it along. So pull up a chair and keep whisking—it will get there eventually.

Preheat the oven to 350°F.

MAKE THE CRUST

1. Mix the graham cracker crumbs, butter, and salt in a large bowl with a fork to form a crumbly mixture that holds together when you pinch it. Pour the mixture into the pie plate and use your hands to press it firmly along the bottom and sides of the plate to form a thick, even crust.

2. Bake the crust for 5 to 7 minutes, until it is just set. Remove the crust from the oven and immediately sprinkle the chocolate evenly over the hot crust. Cover the crust lightly with foil, so that the chocolate melts.

continued

FOR THE FILLING

¼ cup cornstarch

½ cup granulated sugar

¼ teaspoon kosher salt

2 cups whole milk

4 egg yolks (reserve the egg whites for the meringue)

2 tablespoons creamy salted peanut butter

1 tablespoon unsalted butter

½ teaspoon pure vanilla extract

FOR THE MERINGUE

4 egg whites

¼ teaspoon cream of tartar

¼ cup granulated sugar

SPECIAL TOOLS

9-inch deep-dish pie plate

MAKE THE CRUMBLE

Put the powdered sugar, peanut butter, and cinnamon in a medium bowl and use two knives to cut the ingredients together until they've formed a uniform, crumbly mixture.

MAKE THE FILLING

1. Whisk the cornstarch, sugar, and salt in a medium bowl. Heat the milk in a small saucepan over medium heat until it is just steaming. Pour the milk slowly into the cornstarch mixture, whisking as you pour.

2. Heat water in a double boiler (or a large heatproof bowl set over a pot of water) over medium heat until it is steaming. Put the egg yolks into the double boiler and whisk them for just 30 seconds, making sure to scrape the corners and sides well. Slowly pour the milk mixture into the eggs, whisking as you pour.

3. Cook the mixture, whisking constantly, until the custard is very thick, like pudding; this can take anywhere from 5 to 25 minutes.

4. Remove the custard from the heat and stir in the peanut butter, butter, and vanilla until smooth.

5. Spoon two-thirds of the peanut crumble into the pie crust, then pour the hot custard over it. Smooth the top of the custard with the back of your spoon or a spatula.

MAKE THE MERINGUE

1. Put the egg whites into the bowl of a stand mixer fitted with the whisk attachment or a large bowl (if using a hand mixer) and whip them on medium speed until glossy and smooth, about 1 minute. With the mixer still running, add the cream of tartar, then add the sugar, 1 tablespoon at a time, allowing each spoonful to dissolve into the egg whites before adding the next one. Stop the mixer and scrape the bottom and sides of the bowl with a rubber spatula. Turn the mixer to high speed and whip the egg whites until they have stiff peaks, about 1 minute.

2. Pile the meringue on top of the custard, using the rubber spatula to smooth it all the way to the edges of the crust and form whorls.

3. Bake the pie for about 10 minutes, until the edges of the meringue turn brown. Let the pie cool to room temperature on the counter, about 1 hour.

4. Sprinkle the rest of the peanut crumble on top of the meringue, then refrigerate the pie for at least 3 hours or (preferably) overnight to set the custard. The pie can be refrigerated, covered, for 2 to 3 days.

GARDEN HARVEST FEAST

PLUM, FIG, AND ARUGULA CAPRESE SALAD · 187

LEMON BUTTERMILK FRIED CHICKEN
DRIZZLED WITH HONEY · 189

QUICK-PICKLED DILLY BEANS · 191

QUICK-PICKLED SWEET RELISH · 192

SWEET CORN POLENTA · 195

EGGPLANT AND SUMMER SQUASH PARMESAN · 197

PEACH BUCKLE WITH BOURBON WHIPPED CREAM · 201

THERE ARE KITCHEN GARDENS ALL OVER THE RANCH. PRETTY

much everyone who lives here has their own small plot of vegetables and herbs near their house. But the biggest is the shared community vegetable garden behind the Casa. This garden has been planted here for generations, and different family members and friends have taken charge of it over the years. Recently, my dear friend Katie has been leading the process of planning and managing the garden. She's amazing with plants (a quality she gets from her mom, who is a botanist), and she and I really enjoy working together to plan and plant and care for the garden.

We start talking about the garden in the winter, when the seed catalogs arrive. Some girls grow up with teen magazines, but we grew up with seed catalogs, and it's still exciting when they land in our mailboxes. We always order our favorite varieties—things like Cherokee Purple tomatoes and Blue Hubbard heirloom squash—but we like to try out some new (to us) types every year. We also take an inventory of the seeds we've saved from previous years, then plan the garden plots, making sure that we rotate the placement of the different kinds of vegetables so that the soil gets the nutrients it needs and stays fertile year after year.

The real organization starts in the spring, when we work the ground. Katie has an old 8N tractor, which she inherited from her grandfather, and the ranch also has a 1950s 8N; we like to joke that the tractors are siblings, and it's fun to use them side by side. The ideal time to do this is right before the last rains of the season, so that the ground is loose and the soil can hold on to that last bit of moisture. This is also when we plant starts (seedlings) for summer vegetables, such as tomatoes and peppers. I put some trays in warm spots in my house, and Katie grows many in her beautiful greenhouse, which was built by a neighbor years ago out of old windows.

The first planting doesn't happen until we're sure we've seen the last frost of the year. My great-uncle Dibbs used to say that you should put your starts in the ground on May 1. Waiting this long is necessary but can also be frustrating, and we are always eager to get going. We usually schedule a big planting day and let everyone who lives on the ranch know. Many of these friends and family members like to come help and will keep working in the garden all summer, whenever they have time. They can also harvest vegetables for their tables all season long.

Throughout the summer, Katie and I work in the garden when we can—both together and separately—weeding, planting, and making sure none of the water lines get gnawed by menacing gophers. And in return, the garden gives us tons of vegetables to feed our families. This year, we have planted about an acre: There are watermelons and cucumbers, various kinds of zucchini and summer squash, and an entire row of big, bushy Italian basil. We have seven long rows of tomatoes, including small golden cherry tomatoes, pretty green-and-red-striped heirloom varieties, and, of course, lots of Romas for canning and making tomato sauce. There are also three rows of peppers—including poblanos, bell peppers, and shishitos—lots of corn, and a pumpkin patch full of winter squash and carvers for the kids to enjoy at Halloween.

Interspersed throughout the vegetables are rows of colorful edible flowers like nasturtiums, marigolds, and zinnias. These flowers attract pollinators and keep lots of different kinds of pests away, but we also use them in our salads and on cakes and other dishes—pretty much anywhere we want to add a little color. We also have overgrown rosemary bushes and old grapevines all along the fences at the edge of the garden, and nearby there are a couple of small orchards that our cousin Rick prunes every year, which bear apricots, peaches, plums, figs, and pears.

All the vegetables ripen at different times throughout the summer, of course, and when a row or patch of a particular kind of fruit or vegetable ripens all at once, we do what farmers have done for generations: we get out our canning pots. Throughout the summer, if you walk into a kitchen around the ranch, you're very likely to find someone cutting or cooking or portioning mountains of produce. We make jams out of strawberries, blackberries, and apricots; pickle beans and cucumbers and carrots; turn corn and peppers into succotash; and peel ripe tomatoes for sauce. By the end of the season, our pantries are bursting with jars of delicious things.

ψ

The early fall is one of the most abundant times of year in the garden—and also its last hurrah. This season can get really hot, which helps ripen the last of the vegetables, but once the first frost comes, most of the garden will shut down overnight and everything except cold-weather vegetables, like hearty winter squash, will die. So in September and October, we harvest as much as we can.

This is also when I think the garden is at its most beautiful. In the evenings, the light is rich and golden and makes everything almost seem to glow. Katie and I have always talked about having a dinner right in the middle of the rows during this peak season, so this year we invited friends to come over to pick some of the year's last vegetables for themselves and enjoy an early dinner. The first to arrive is our longtime friend Blakeney Sanford, an incredible artist who grew up just on the other side of these hills. Her father, Richard Sanford, was one of the first winemakers to popularize growing and making wine in Santa Barbara County, so she had a similar agricultural upbringing just a few hills away.

For dinner, I make a bunch of beautiful, flavorful dishes that highlight the food at its best in the garden right now. I start by assembling a caprese-style salad made with plums and figs in place of the usual tomatoes and tuck them into little nests of arugula. Then there's my light, summery take on eggplant parmesan (which I make with both eggplant and summer squash) and a comforting pot of polenta sweetened with fresh corn. I also make crispy fried chicken drizzled with ranch honey. Dessert will be a simple but flavorful peach buckle.

Together, we carry an old picnic table into the field and find a good sunny spot between the tomatoes and the winter squash. Everyone passes the food around the table, serving each other from big platters and pots. When the plates are full, we call to the kids, who are running through the rows of vegetables, and settle down to a beautiful end-of-season dinner.

PLUM, FIG, *and* ARUGULA CAPRESE SALAD

ACTIVE TIME
15 minutes

TOTAL TIME
15 minutes

SERVES
6

3 large ripe but firm red plums, like Santa Rosas or elephant hearts

3 large figs

One 8-ounce ball fresh mozzarella

2 cups loosely packed basil leaves

4 cups loosely packed arugula

¼ cup freshly squeezed lemon juice

¼ cup extra virgin olive oil

½ teaspoon kosher salt

¼ cup Balsamic Glaze (page 175) or store-bought

Maldon salt or other flaky sea salt

This is the perfect late-summer salad, and it highlights all the best fruits that grow on the ranch at this time of year. Tangy plums, sweet figs, creamy mozzarella, and peppery arugula complement each other with every bite. It's also quite an elegant salad. I make it in individual portions (even though I keep them all together, on a big platter), and the stacks of fruit and cheese are gorgeous tucked into little nests of greens. Even better, because you don't toss the ingredients together or scoop them up from a big bowl, this salad stays beautiful as you serve it.

1. Halve and pit the plums, then cut the halves into very thin wedges, about ⅓ inch thick. Quarter the figs lengthwise. Cut the mozzarella into ¼-inch-thick slices, then cut each slice in half to form semicircles. Tear each basil leaf in half crosswise.

2. Mix the basil and the arugula in a large bowl, add the lemon juice, olive oil, and salt, and toss everything together.

3. Divide the greens into 6 even portions and form them into little nests on a serving plate. Make a stack of one semicircle of mozzarella, a couple of slices of plum, a second semicircle of mozzarella, and another couple of plum slices; you'll have 2 layers of cheese and 2 layers of plum. Nestle this stack into the center of one of the portions of greens and top with 2 pieces of fig.

4. Repeat this process 5 more times, for a total of 6 salad nests. Drizzle 2 teaspoons of the balsamic glaze on top of each stack and sprinkle on a pinch of the flaky salt. Serve the nests using a spatula.

LEMON BUTTERMILK FRIED CHICKEN DRIZZLED *with* HONEY

ACTIVE TIME
1 hour

TOTAL TIME
4 hours, including brining (or longer if you brine all day)

SERVES
4

FOR THE BRINE

2 tablespoons extra virgin olive oil

5 garlic cloves, roughly chopped

½ yellow onion, sliced

2 tablespoons kosher salt

2 tablespoons fresh rosemary leaves

5 lemons

4 cups water

FOR THE CHICKEN

8 chicken drumsticks

2 cups all-purpose flour

2 tablespoons kosher salt

2 tablespoons ground black pepper

2 tablespoons onion powder

2 tablespoons sweet paprika

When I make fried chicken, I brine drumsticks in a mixture that has lots of rosemary and lemon to add a distinctive California flavor, then I drizzle honey on the chicken just before serving. If you've never deep-fried anything before, the process might seem intimidating, but once you try it, you'll see that it's very straightforward. The trick for me is to get my cooking station organized before I start: I prepare my flour mixture and pour my buttermilk into a bowl and set them on the counter next to the stove, and I have tongs and a potholder or oven mitts nearby. That way, when I start frying, I won't have to walk away from the stove or go looking for something; I can just focus on cooking.

BRINE THE CHICKEN

1. Combine the olive oil, garlic, and onion in a Dutch oven or heavy-duty pot, season it with the salt, and cook everything over low heat until the onion is golden brown, about 10 minutes. Add the rosemary to the pot. Cut the lemons in half, squeeze their juice into the pot (seeds and all), and add the lemon halves too.

2. Cook until the lemons have heated through and you can smell them but the lemon juice has not evaporated, about 5 minutes. Add the water and bring the mixture to a simmer. Simmer the brine for about 30 minutes, then turn off the heat and transfer the brine (including the lemon halves) to a heatproof container. Refrigerate it until it's cool, about 30 minutes.

3. Put the chicken legs in a nonreactive container and pour the brine on top of them. Make sure the chicken is completely submerged in the liquid, cover the container, and refrigerate the mixture for at least 2 hours, preferably more (up to 10), to flavor the meat.

FRY THE CHICKEN

1. Mix the flour, salt, pepper, onion powder, paprika, and baking powder in a medium bowl. Pour the buttermilk into a separate medium bowl. Remove the chicken from the brine and pat it dry with paper towels. Dredge the pieces of chicken in the flour mixture, making sure to coat all sides, and set them on a plate or a cooling rack set into a sheet pan.

continued

2 tablespoons baking powder

3 cups reduced-fat buttermilk

6 cups vegetable oil

Honey

SPECIAL TOOLS

Deep-fry thermometer

2. Pour the vegetable oil into a Dutch oven or heavy, deep-sided pot with a deep-fry thermometer attached to the side. Heat the oil over medium heat until it reaches 350°F.

3. Working in batches, dip each drumstick into the bowl of buttermilk, making sure to cover it completely, dip it back into the flour mixture, turning to coat it, and then carefully place it into the hot oil. (You'll be able to fit 3 to 4 legs in the pot at a time; make sure not to crowd the pieces or let the oil get too close to the top of the pot.) Fry the chicken, turning each piece with tongs as necessary, until it's crisp and lightly browned, about 7 minutes. Remove the pieces from the pot with tongs and place them on a plate lined with paper towels or on a clean cooling rack set on a sheet pan. Let the oil come back to 350°F and repeat the process with another batch of chicken. (If your chicken is on a cooling rack, you can put it into the oven, at 250°F, to keep it warm.)

4. Drizzle the chicken lightly with honey before serving.

TIP: If you double this recipe, you'll want to switch to new oil for the second batch.

QUICK-PICKLED DILLY BEANS

ACTIVE TIME
25 minutes

TOTAL TIME
*1 week, including
pickling*

MAKES
6 half-pint jars

FOR THE BRINE

2 cups water

1 cup unseasoned rice
vinegar

3 tablespoons distilled
white vinegar

6 tablespoons granulated
sugar

3 tablespoons kosher salt

FOR THE PICKLES

12 garlic cloves

6 teaspoons black
peppercorns

3 teaspoons mustard
seeds

3 teaspoons coriander
seeds

18 large fresh dill sprigs

1 to 2 pounds green beans,
trimmed

SPECIAL TOOLS

6 half-pint jars with
matching lids and rings

Making quick pickles—which you keep in the refrigerator, instead of canning—is a simple and convenient way to make vegetables last just a little longer. Anyone can do it (including kids), so it's a good way to try your hand at preserving. This was one of the first recipes Katie and I created when we started teaching Ranch Table classes at the Casa, and it's still one of my favorite things to demonstrate. Feel free to play with the spices you add to the jars to give different flavors to your pickles. If you like heat, for instance, you could add some red pepper flakes. Have fun with it!

I serve these as a side with all kinds of foods, set them out in bowls for guests to nibble on before meals, and put them in Micheladas (page 43).

MAKE THE BRINE

1. Bring the water to a boil in a medium saucepan over high heat. Add the vinegars, sugar, and salt and stir until everything has dissolved, 2 to 5 minutes. Set the brine aside to cool to room temperature.

2. Prepare the jars and lids by washing them in hot, soapy water and letting them dry.

ASSEMBLE THE JARS

1. Put 2 garlic cloves, 1 teaspoon of the black peppercorns, ½ teaspoon of the mustard seeds, ½ teaspoon of the coriander seeds, and 3 fresh dill sprigs in each jar. Divide the green beans into 6 bundles (about 20 to 25 beans in each) and put them in the jars, standing them upright; the ends should stick up toward the tops of the jars. (Cut in half any that don't fit.)

2. Pour the cooled brine into the jars, making sure you add enough to cover the beans. Put the lids and rings on the jars and mark each jar with the date.

3. Refrigerate the jars for at least 1 week before using; enjoy the pickles within 1 month.

QUICK-PICKLED SWEET RELISH

ACTIVE TIME
20 minutes

TOTAL TIME
1 hour 20 minutes

MAKES
1 half-pint jar

2 cucumbers, roughly chopped (about 1½ pounds)

1 medium sweet onion, such as Vidalia or Walla Walla, roughly chopped

1 tablespoon kosher salt

½ cup white vinegar

½ cup granulated sugar

SPECIAL TOOLS

1 half-pint jar with matching lid and ring

Every summer, my mom and I spend a ton of time making preserves. When I was growing up, I'd spend hours helping her as she made succotash, relishes, canned tomatoes, bread-and-butter pickles, pepper jelly, and all kinds of other things on her 1950s Wedgewood stove. She gave away plenty of what she made, but she also has a wall of shelves in her kitchen just for jars of preserves, and we'd use them all year long. Today, I follow my mom's lead, and recently (when I got tired of having stacks of canned goods everywhere), I too added a huge wall of shelves in my pantry to keep everything handy. This relish, which I love to make, works just as well in the refrigerator, so you don't have to get a canning pot to enjoy it.

1. Put the cucumbers and onion in a food processor and pulse until they're the size you like for relish; this can range from finely to very finely chopped.

2. Pour the cucumber mixture into a fine-mesh sieve, mix in the salt, and set the sieve over a bowl. Cover the sieve with a cloth and let the vegetables sit for 1 hour so that the salt can draw moisture out of them.

3. Prepare the jar and lid by washing them in hot, soapy water and letting them dry.

4. Bring the vinegar to a boil in a medium saucepan over high heat. Add the sugar and stir until it has dissolved. Once the mixture returns to a boil, continue boiling until it has thickened and reduced by half, about 4 minutes.

5. In the meantime, pour the cucumber mixture into a clean kitchen towel and squeeze it over the sink to remove as much moisture as possible. When the vinegar has reduced, add the cucumber mixture and stir until well combined.

6. Transfer the mixture to the half-pint jar. Put the lid and ring on the jar and mark it with the date.

7. Refrigerate the jar and enjoy right away or within 1 month.

SWEET CORN POLENTA

ACTIVE TIME
45 minutes

TOTAL TIME
1 hour

SERVES
6 to 8

5 cups water

1½ teaspoons kosher salt

1 cup ground cornmeal or polenta

1 cup fresh or frozen and thawed corn kernels (from 1 ear)

½ cup heavy cream

¼ cup (½ stick) unsalted butter

1 cup freshly grated Parmesan

¼ teaspoon ground black pepper

Polenta is creamy and filling and comforting—the perfect accompaniment for dishes with sauce, like braised meats or my cheesy, tomatoey Eggplant and Summer Squash Parmesan (page 197). I really like putting fresh corn into my polenta in the summer (or frozen kernels in winter), because it adds a sweet pop of flavor to every bite. Then I finish it with a big pile of Parmesan, which rounds out the flavor with a bit of savoriness and a hint of salt.

1. Bring the water and ½ teaspoon of the salt to a boil in a large Dutch oven or heavy-duty pot.

2. Add the cornmeal and mix well with a wooden spoon for 5 minutes, cover, and cook over low heat for 25 minutes.

3. Uncover and add the corn, cream, and butter and continue to cook on low, stirring constantly, until the cornmeal is fully cooked through and creamy, 10 to 15 more minutes.

4. Remove the pot from the heat, then stir in the parmesan, pepper, and remaining teaspoon salt.

EGGPLANT *and* SUMMER SQUASH PARMESAN

ACTIVE TIME
30 minutes

TOTAL TIME
2 hours

SERVES
6 to 8

2 large Italian eggplants
(3½ pounds)

1¾ cups extra virgin olive
oil

2 teaspoons kosher salt

6 to 7 medium zucchini
or other summer squash
(3½ pounds)

3 garlic cloves

½ cup tightly packed basil
leaves

½ cup tightly packed flat-
leaf parsley

½ cup freshly grated
Parmesan

2 cups panko bread
crumbs

1 pound part-skim
mozzarella

2 cups Quick Marinara
(page 99) or store-bought

My friend Julia and I developed this dish for Ranch Table events. It isn't a traditional eggplant parmesan; we don't fry the sliced eggplant or give it a thick coat of breading. Instead, we bake both eggplant and summer squash until they're tender and golden, and then layer them in a casserole dish with marinara sauce and mozzarella. The breading comes as a layer on top of the entire dish, and it bakes to a nice golden brown. This way, we get all the deliciousness of the classic version of the dish but with a lot less effort. (In fact, you don't even have to salt the eggplant; it releases its moisture as it roasts.)

1. Preheat the oven to 400°F.

2. Trim the eggplants and cut them lengthwise into ½-inch-thick slices. Grease two sheet pans with 2 tablespoons of the olive oil per pan. Lay the eggplant slices on the sheets, pour another 2 tablespoons of olive oil over them on each pan, then sprinkle each pan with ¼ teaspoon of the salt. Roast the slices for 15 to 20 minutes, until the bottoms are golden brown. Flip the eggplant slices over and continue roasting for another 10 minutes. Stack the eggplant on a large plate.

3. Trim the squash and cut them lengthwise into ⅓-inch-thick slices. Grease each sheet pan with 2 more tablespoons of olive oil per pan. Lay the squash slices on the sheets, pour another 2 tablespoons of olive oil onto them on each pan, and sprinkle each pan with ¼ teaspoon of the salt. Roast the slices for 15 to 20 minutes, until the bottoms are golden brown. Flip the slices over and continue roasting for another 10 minutes.

4. While the squash is roasting, put 1 garlic clove, the basil, parsley, 1 teaspoon of the salt, and ¼ cup of the olive oil in a food processor and pulse until everything is finely chopped and well mixed. Add the Parmesan and pulse until combined.

5. Pour the panko into a medium bowl, add the herb mixture and the remaining ½ cup olive oil, and mix well.

6. Reduce the oven temperature to 350°F. Cut the remaining 2 garlic cloves into very thin slices and cut the mozzarella into slices about ⅛ inch thick.

continued

7. Spread ½ cup of the marinara on the bottom of a 9 × 13-inch baking dish. Lay half the eggplant over it in a relatively even layer. Layer one-third of the mozzarella slices on top of the eggplant, then scatter one-third of the sliced garlic evenly over the mozzarella.

8. Spread another ½ cup of marinara over the casserole, lay half the squash over it in a relatively even layer, and layer on another one-third of the mozzarella and one-third of the garlic.

9. Repeat the layering above with another ½ cup of marinara, the remaining eggplant, and the remaining mozzarella. Spread the remaining ½ cup marinara over the casserole, then place the rest of the squash as a final layer on top.

10. Pack the panko mixture into the baking dish in a thick layer on top of the vegetables.

11. Place the baking dish onto a sheet pan. Bake the casserole for 40 to 50 minutes, until the top is golden brown.

12. Let it cool for 5 to 10 minutes so that the cheese firms up just a bit. Cut it into squares with a spatula to serve.

PEACH BUCKLE *with* BOURBON WHIPPED CREAM

ACTIVE TIME
30 minutes

TOTAL TIME
1 hour 45 minutes

SERVES
6 to 8

FOR THE BUCKLE

6 to 8 peaches (2 pounds)

2¼ cups granulated sugar

1½ cups all-purpose flour

1½ tablespoons baking powder

1 teaspoon kosher salt

½ teaspoon ground cinnamon

1½ cups whole milk

1 teaspoon pure vanilla extract

1 cup (2 sticks) unsalted butter

FOR THE WHIPPED CREAM

2 cups heavy cream

½ cup granulated sugar

2 teaspoons bourbon or pure vanilla extract

I love a classic, old-fashioned buckle. It's really easy to make, and the combination of cooked fruit with the sweet, puffy, crunchy, and almost chewy crust is just the best. When I make this, I think of one of my godmothers, Sarah, who reintroduced me to this dessert when she visited one summer. The great part about a buckle is that you scatter the fruit on top of the batter, and as it bakes, it collapses—or "buckles"—into the dish, and the batter rises up around it. You can make this with any soft fruit, but in summer I really love to use sweet, juicy peaches.

MAKE THE BUCKLE

1. Preheat the oven to 350°F.

2. Halve and pit the peaches, then cut them into ½-inch-thick slices. (There's no need to peel them.) Gently toss the peaches with ¼ cup of the sugar; set them aside.

3. Mix the flour, the remaining 2 cups sugar, the baking powder, salt, and cinnamon in a large bowl. Add the milk and vanilla and stir with a wooden spoon until well combined, 2 to 3 minutes.

4. Put the butter into a 9 × 13-inch baking dish and bake for about 10 minutes, until the butter melts; be sure to take it out before the butter starts to brown. Pour the batter over the melted butter and distribute the peaches over the batter.

5. Return the pan to the oven and bake the buckle for 1 hour. When the top is golden brown, cover the pan with foil, taking care to leave space between the buckle and the foil in case the cake continues to rise. Return the pan to the oven and bake for another 15 minutes, until a toothpick inserted into the center comes out clean. Let the buckle cool for 20 minutes.

MAKE THE WHIPPED CREAM

1. Pour the cream into the bowl of a stand mixer fitted with the whisk attachment and whip it on medium speed until it begins to hold soft peaks. Add the sugar and the bourbon and whip for 1 more minute. (Alternatively, whisk the cream with a hand mixer in a large bowl.)

2. Serve the buckle warm with the whipped cream.

CIDER PRESS POTLUCK

TURKEY BARLEY SOUP · 209

TURKEY OR CHICKEN BROTH · 210

ROASTED WINTER SQUASH · 213

SWEET BUTTERMILK DINNER ROLLS · 215

with Cranberry Butter 216

made with Ginger-Jalapeño Cranberry Sauce 216

HONEY LEMON CAKE · 217

SPICED HONEY APPLE PIE WITH A GINGER CRUST · 221

MULLED APPLE CIDER · 223

WHEN YOU THINK OF ALL THE TOOLS YOU NEED TO RUN
a cattle ranch, you probably don't think about the importance of a large, sturdy cider press. But on the San Julian, our press is one of our most beloved pieces of equipment. It lives in the old wool barn, by the Casa, along with some rusty antique tools and a black horse buggy that has probably been sitting there for generations. Once a year we pull the press out, wash it off, and host a cider press potluck.

My great-uncle Dibbs started this cider-making party tradition decades ago. There are apple trees planted all over the ranch, some in the orchard below my house, some by the Casa, and some near the old schoolhouse that my grandfather and the other kids on the ranch used to go to. The pressing used to happen on various fall weekends, whenever it was convenient. But as time went on, the trees grew so much and produced so many apples that we needed more people to process them—and to take home some of the cider. So it became a tradition to have the pressing the Saturday after Thanksgiving.

We always have lots of friends and family staying with us at Thanksgiving, and our friends and neighbors have relatives in town for the holiday as well, so we invite a huge crowd to come out to the Casa and join in the fun.

Everyone is asked to bring a dish or two for a potluck buffet lunch, along with some empty wine bottles to fill with cider. These informal, relaxed weekends bring our entire community together and combine our various holiday foods into one big, generous meal. It's a chance to meet everyone's extended family, try the dishes they made for their Thanksgiving tables, and see what they did with their extra turkey—their posoles, soups, enchiladas, potpies, and casseroles. They expand our family's holiday to embrace everyone's rich and varied traditions.

ψ

When my dad was growing up, the family's cider press was the old wooden kind with a big crank on it. You had to put a board in the crank to get enough leverage to crush the apples, and the kids would work together and push on the board to turn it. I remember using this same press when I was a little kid, but sometime in the 1990s, Dibbs replaced it with a newer machine, and that's the one we use today. It has an electric motor attached to a grinder that turns the apples into pulp and a hydraulic lever that makes it easy to lower the pressing plate down onto that pulp to extract the juice.

This year, we enlist Jack's help to pull this enormous contraption out of the barn. He backs the four-wheeler into the dim, dusty space; connects it to the front of the press, which has its own wheels; then slowly pulls it across the road and through the gate so that we can set it up in a sunny spot next to the Casa, next to an old pomegranate tree.

When the equipment is safely in its place, Austin and I take the truck down the road to the hay barn to get some large picnic tables for lunch. We set them up under our small grove of towering redwood trees, and I decorate them with some splitting pomegranates still on their branches and golden grape leaves from the arbor on the other side of the house. It takes only a couple of minutes to add these small touches, but the casual decorations give the whole space a festive, holiday feel.

The apples, which everyone helped pick over the past few weeks, are sitting in big boxes in the old cooler—a refrigerated portion of an outbuilding lined with cedar, where we store produce from the garden. The room smells sweet and musty, a mix of cedar and aging apples. We haul the heavy boxes out to a table near the cider press and pour the apples into big, galvanized buckets filled with water. The fruit floats and bobs, shining and colorful in the bright morning light, and the water is bitingly cold on my fingers as I stir them to make sure everything is well rinsed. The chill in the air and the water and the reds and yellows of the fruit are a visceral reminder that even on the sunny Central Coast, fall can feel like its own distinct season, a brief moment of slanted golden light and brilliant color before the frosts and rains of winter.

When most of our guests have arrived, we get to work: a dozen people or so gather around the work tables, grab knives, and start cutting the apples into large chunks. The kids are the most enthusiastic cutters at first, eagerly chopping away. But as soon as the motor on the grinder starts up, they crowd around the cider press, and the adults take over. Processing all the apples will take the better part of the morning, and everyone here knows that this is a hands-on workday, even if the atmosphere feels like a party.

When a large bucketful of apples has been cut, Jack climbs to the top of a ladder so he can stand over the chute, and starts throwing the fruit into the grinder, bit by bit. Everything goes in, stems and cores included, and comes out as a rough mash. When there's a nice pile, Austin wraps it up in burlap and sets it between two wooden pressing plates, and Jack climbs down to work the small, manual handle on the hydraulic press. As the mash is crushed, golden juice pours out of the bottom of the press into a large pitcher, and the air around us starts to smell sweet. When the jug is filled, it's replaced with a clean one, and my parents and I start filling friends' wine bottles with the golden elixir.

This process repeats all morning; the adults rotate through the stations, and every kid gets a turn to throw the apples down the chute and work the press. The last to go is Katie's little boy, Bobby, who marches sturdily up the ladder and throws his apple slices with the most serious, purposeful look I've ever seen, earning shouts of encouragement from the adults around him.

When the cider is finally pressed, it's time for lunch. All the food is laid out, and we help ourselves to a little bit of everything that looks good. There are large, vinegary salads topped with shredded turkey and dried cranberries. I've made a big pot of turkey barley soup, buttermilk dinner rolls with cranberry butter, roasted winter squash, honey lemon cake, and a spiced apple pie with a sweet ginger crust. Having everyone's dishes all on one table makes for a crazy kind of menu, but it also makes for a very meaningful meal, and for that I am grateful.

TURKEY BARLEY SOUP

ACTIVE TIME
15 minutes

TOTAL TIME
50 minutes

SERVES
4 to 6

¼ cup (½ stick) unsalted butter

1 sweet onion, such as Vidalia or Walla Walla, roughly chopped

1 teaspoon kosher salt, plus more to taste

1 cup peeled small-diced carrots

½ cup small-diced celery

2 garlic cloves, finely chopped

1 teaspoon fresh thyme leaves

8 cups (2 quarts) Turkey or Chicken Broth (page 210) or store-bought

1 cup pearled barley

2 cups chopped roast turkey or chicken

2 bay leaves

Chopped cabbage, sliced radishes, lemon wedges, and hot sauce (optional)

One of my favorite ways to use up extra turkey after Thanksgiving is to make a big pot of this soup. My dad grew barley on the ranch when I was growing up, and I have great memories of sitting on his massive green harvester with him. If you want to make this soup at a different time of year, when you don't have a bunch of leftover turkey sitting around, you can use a roast chicken, or you can roast a bone-in, skin-on turkey breast and use that. The toppings for this soup are basically the same ones you'd add to a posole: fresh, crunchy cabbage and radishes, a good squeeze of lemon or lime, and some hot sauce.

1. Melt the butter in a large Dutch oven or heavy-duty pot over medium heat. Add the onion and salt and cook, stirring frequently, until golden brown, about 5 minutes.

2. Add the carrots, celery, garlic, and thyme to the pot and cook, stirring frequently, until the celery and garlic have softened, about 5 minutes.

3. Add the broth to the pot, turn the heat to high, and bring the soup to a simmer. Add the barley, reduce the heat to low, cover the pot, and continue to simmer the soup, stirring occasionally, until the barley is al dente, about 20 minutes.

4. Add the turkey and bay leaves to the pot and simmer the soup, uncovered, until the carrots and barley are tender, about 10 more minutes. Taste the soup and adjust the seasoning as needed. Remove the bay leaves.

5. To serve, top each bowl with some cabbage and radish and put the lemon wedges and hot sauce (if using) on the side.

TURKEY OR CHICKEN BROTH

ACTIVE TIME
5 minutes

TOTAL TIME
2 to 4 hours

MAKES
about 2 quarts

2 celery stalks

2 carrots

1 yellow onion

1 to 2 pounds roasted
chicken or turkey bones

2 garlic cloves

2 teaspoons kosher salt,
plus more to taste

1 teaspoon whole black
peppercorns

Whenever I roast a chicken or a turkey, I always save the bones to make stock. The roasted bones—and any bits of leftover meat and fat on them—bring tons of flavor. I often make a lot of broth and freeze it to use in the future. The longer you cook the broth, the more flavorful it will be, so I just put it on the back of my stove and keep it simmering for a few hours. If you want to make stock when you don't have leftover bones, you can get chicken backs and wings (or a couple of turkey breasts) from a butcher, roast them with some salt and pepper until they're nice and brown and have reached 165°F (about 30 minutes), and use those bones—you'll also end up with some great meat to add to your soups, too.

1. Cut the celery stalks, carrots, and onion in half crosswise. Put them in a large Dutch oven or stockpot with the bones, garlic, salt, and peppercorns and add 12 to 14 cups of water, enough to cover all the ingredients by about 4 inches.

2. Bring the water to a boil over high heat, then reduce the heat to low. Simmer the stock, uncovered, for anywhere from 2 to 4 hours. (Some water will evaporate, but add more if it recedes below the top of the ingredients.)

3. When the broth is done to your liking, strain it through a colander or sieve to remove the solids. Taste and adjust the seasoning. Let the broth cool a bit so that it's not scalding, then transfer it to heatproof jars and put it in the refrigerator to finish cooling. Use or freeze the broth (in freezer-safe containers) within 3 days.

ROASTED WINTER SQUASH

ACTIVE TIME
10 minutes

TOTAL TIME
*3 hours 10 minutes,
including marinating
(or longer if you
marinate overnight)*

SERVES
4

1 medium kabocha or
other winter squash
(about 3 pounds)

¼ cup finely diced shallot

¼ cup extra virgin olive oil

1 teaspoon orange zest

2 tablespoons freshly
squeezed orange juice

2 tablespoons light brown
sugar

2 teaspoons minced
rosemary leaves

½ teaspoon kosher salt

Ground black pepper

2 teaspoons Maldon salt or
other flaky sea salt

Rosemary flowers
(optional)

*Roast squash is a great side dish to make for a holiday buffet or a big
dinner party because you can make it up to a day in advance. It's
so good hot, right out of the oven, but I also like to serve it at room
temperature. Kabocha is a very sweet squash, so I keep the other
ingredients in this dish pretty simple, to highlight its deliciousness.*

1. Peel the squash with a vegetable peeler or a knife, then cut it in half
lengthwise. Scoop out and discard the seeds and stringy membranes. Cut the
squash into wedges that are roughly 1½ inches at their widest spot.

2. Put the squash in a big zip-top bag or a large container with a lid that
seals well. Add the shallot, olive oil, orange zest, orange juice, brown sugar,
rosemary leaves, salt, and some black pepper, seal the bag or lid, and shake
everything to mix. Marinate the squash for at least 2 hours or (preferably)
overnight, shaking a couple of times to redistribute the marinade.

3. Preheat the oven to 400°F.

4. Arrange the squash (and marinade ingredients) on a sheet pan. Roast the
squash for 45 to 50 minutes, without flipping it, until it is tender when you stick
it with a fork. (The side touching the pan will caramelize slightly.)

5. Transfer the squash to a serving plate and scatter the flaky salt and
rosemary flowers over it (if using).

TIP: This recipe calls for both orange juice and orange zest; make sure to
zest the orange before juicing it.

SWEET BUTTERMILK DINNER ROLLS

ACTIVE TIME
30 minutes

TOTAL TIME
3 hours

MAKES
8 rolls

These dinner rolls are perfect—soft and tender with a golden-brown crust. Adding lots of buttermilk and melted butter to the dough makes them extra fluffy and gives them a warm, rich flavor. They're rich enough to eat on their own, but I like to serve them with flavored butter, like a cranberry butter I make with extra cranberry sauce. (You can use any cranberry sauce you like for the butter recipe; I've included my Ginger-Jalapeño Cranberry Sauce recipe here as an option.)

1 cup reduced-fat buttermilk

¼ cup (½ stick) unsalted butter

2½ cups all-purpose flour, plus more for dusting

1 packet (2¼ teaspoons) instant yeast

2 teaspoons granulated sugar

½ teaspoon baking soda

1 teaspoon kosher salt

Extra virgin olive oil, for greasing

1 large egg

Maldon salt or other flaky sea salt (optional)

Cranberry Butter (recipe follows)

1. Combine the buttermilk and butter in a medium saucepan and heat them over medium heat until the mixture is just steaming (around 115°F); cover the pot to keep the mixture warm. Set aside.

2. Put 1½ cups of the flour, the yeast, sugar, baking soda, and salt in the bowl of a stand mixer fitted with the dough hook or a large bowl (if using a hand mixer) and mix thoroughly. Turn the mixer on low speed, then slowly pour the buttermilk mixture into the flour. Add the remaining 1 cup flour to the bowl and mix on medium speed until the dough begins to stick together, about 5 minutes.

3. Transfer the dough to a lightly floured surface and knead until it is very smooth, about 10 minutes.

4. Grease a large bowl with olive oil. Shape the dough into a ball, place it in the bowl, and cover the bowl with plastic wrap. Set the bowl in a warm spot and let the dough rise until it has doubled, about 2 hours.

5. Use your fist to gently punch the dough down, then transfer it to a lightly floured surface. Divide the dough into 8 pieces and knead each piece individually for about 1 minute.

6. Line a sheet pan with parchment paper. Roll each piece of dough into a ball, then place all the balls onto the prepared sheet pan in two rows of 4. Cover the balls lightly with plastic wrap and let them rise in a warm spot until they start to look light and puffy, about 15 minutes.

7. In the meantime, preheat the oven to 400°F.

8. Whisk the egg well in a small bowl. Uncover the rolls and use a pastry brush to brush them very gently with the egg. Sprinkle them with a large pinch of sea salt (if using).

9. Bake the rolls for 10 to 15 minutes, until the tops are golden brown. Serve them warm with cranberry butter.

CRANBERRY BUTTER

½ cup salted butter, at room temperature

2 tablespoons Ginger-Jalapeño Cranberry Sauce (below) or cranberry sauce of your choice

ACTIVE TIME	TOTAL TIME	MAKES
3 minutes	*3 minutes*	*½ cup*

Put the butter in a small bowl, add the cranberry sauce, and mash everything together with a fork until it's well combined. Refrigerate until serving.

GINGER-JALAPENO CRANBERRY SAUCE

One 12-ounce bag cranberries, picked through

1½ cups granulated sugar

1 cup water

½ cup freshly squeezed orange juice

1 teaspoon ground ginger

1 jalapeño, seeded

ACTIVE TIME	TOTAL TIME	MAKES
25 minutes	*45 minutes, including cooling*	*2 cups*

1. Put the cranberries, sugar, water, orange juice, ginger, and jalapeño in a medium saucepan. Bring everything to a boil over high heat.

2. Reduce the heat and let the mixture simmer; as the cranberries start to soften and pop, mash them against the side of the pan with a wooden spoon. Continue cooking until the sauce thickens, 10 to 15 minutes.

3. Remove the jalapeño and let the sauce cool to room temperature. Refrigerate for up to a week.

HONEY LEMON CAKE

ACTIVE TIME
20 minutes

My honey lemon cake is as simple as it is delicious. Everything gets mixed together in one bowl, and it bakes in a regular round cake pan. But while it's easy to make, a little bit of glaze on top, a scattering of bee pollen, and some edible flowers make it feel really special. My favorite thing about this cake is the honey, which gives it all its sweetness and makes it rich and dense. Because the honey adds so much flavor, changing the type of honey you use will also change the flavor a bit. I always make this cake with the wildflower-and-sage honey from the ranch, but you could try it with another kind of honey with a distinctive flavor, like orange blossom.

ACTIVE TIME
20 minutes

TOTAL TIME
1 hour 20 minutes

SERVES
6 to 8

FOR THE CAKE

2½ cups all-purpose flour

1½ teaspoons baking powder

1 teaspoon kosher salt

1 cup (2 sticks) unsalted butter, at room temperature

3 large eggs

1 cup whole milk

1 teaspoon pure vanilla extract

1 teaspoon finely grated lemon zest

1 teaspoon freshly squeezed lemon juice

1 cup honey

Vegetable oil, for greasing

1 tablespoon dried bee pollen (optional)

Marigolds, sage flowers, or other edible flowers (optional)

MAKE THE CAKE

1. Preheat the oven to 350°F.

2. Sift the flour into a large bowl and mix in the baking powder and salt; set the mixture aside.

3. Put the butter and eggs into the bowl of a stand mixer fitted with the paddle attachment or a large bowl (if using a hand mixer) and beat until the mixture is whipped and fluffy, about 2 minutes. Add the milk, vanilla, lemon zest, and lemon juice and beat until everything is well mixed.

4. Add about one-third of the flour mixture to the bowl and mix until just incorporated; scrape down the sides of the bowl with a rubber spatula. Repeat the process two more times to add the remaining flour mixture. Slowly pour the honey into the batter and gently mix and fold it in until it is thoroughly incorporated.

5. Grease the cake pan with the oil, making sure to cover the bottom and sides well. Pour the batter into the prepared pan and smooth it out with the rubber spatula.

6. Bake the cake for about 45 minutes, until a tester inserted into the center comes out clean.

7. Let the cake cool in the pan for 15 minutes, then flip it onto a cooling rack and let it continue cooling upside down.

continued

FOR THE LEMON GLAZE

2½ cups powdered sugar, sifted

½ cup freshly squeezed lemon juice

SPECIAL TOOLS

One 8-inch-round cake pan

Mortar and pestle (optional)

MAKE THE GLAZE

1. Put the powdered sugar into a medium bowl, then drizzle in the lemon juice, whisking the mixture slowly until it is fluid and drips easily.

2. With the cake still on the cooling rack, gently pour the glaze over it, so that it sits on top of the cake and drips naturally over the sides. (Using the bottom of the cake as the top will give it a nice flat surface.) Transfer the cake to a serving plate.

3. Put the bee pollen (if using) into a mortar and mash it with a pestle into a fine powder, then scatter big pinches of it onto the glaze. Arrange the edible flowers (if using) around the edges of the cake.

SPICED HONEY APPLE PIE
with A GINGER CRUST

ACTIVE TIME
30 minutes

TOTAL TIME
3 hours, including cooling time

SERVES
6 to 8

¼ cup all-purpose flour, plus more for dusting

Ginger Pie Crust (see the variation on page 70)

6 Gravenstein or Granny Smith apples (3½ to 4 pounds)

2 tablespoons freshly squeezed lemon juice

¼ cup granulated sugar

1 teaspoon ground cinnamon

½ teaspoon ground ginger

¼ teaspoon ground cloves

¼ cup honey

2 tablespoons unsalted butter

1 large egg

1 tablespoon turbinado sugar

SPECIAL TOOLS

9-inch deep-dish pie plate

A big apple pie is the perfect fall dessert, and I like to make mine really tall, with lots and lots of apples piled up in a mound under a crisp, flaky crust. Ugly apples are the best for making pies since you can cut out any bad parts. I save these apples from our trees just for pie, and also buy up the seconds at the farmers' market. We grow Gravenstein apples on the ranch, but you can use any other firm, tart apples. I also like to make my apple pies in a ginger crust, because I would eat ginger every day if I could, and the flavors go so well together.

1. Preheat the oven to 350°F.

2. On a lightly floured surface, roll out one of the pieces of pie crust dough into a ¼-inch-thick circle that is 16 inches in diameter. (Keep the other piece of dough in the refrigerator.) Transfer the dough to the pie plate. (If it's hanging over the edges by more than ½ inch, trim it.) Refrigerate the dough.

3. Peel and core the apples and cut them into ½-inch-thick slices (you'll have about 10 cups). Put the slices into a large bowl with the lemon juice, granulated sugar, flour, cinnamon, ginger, and cloves; mix well.

4. Remove the pie plate from refrigerator and pour the apples into the pie crust, mounding them up in the center. Drizzle the honey over the top. Cut the butter into ½-inch pieces and scatter it across the filling.

5. Remove the other half of the crust from the refrigerator. On a lightly floured surface, roll the pie crust dough out into a ¼-inch-thick circle. Lay it on top of the pie and tuck the edges of both the upper and lower crusts under the lower crust, then pinch the dough shut.

6. Cut a small hole in the center of the crust with a paring knife, then cut five vents, each about 2 inches long, radiating out from the center of the pie (to mirror the star shape you get when you cut an apple in half horizontally). Whisk the egg in a small bowl and brush it over the top of the pie with a pastry brush, then sprinkle the turbinado sugar evenly over the crust.

7. Bake the pie for 50 to 60 minutes, until the top is golden brown and the sugar has begun to caramelize. (If the crust starts to brown too much, cover it with a piece of aluminum foil.) Let the pie cool for at least 15 minutes.

MULLED APPLE CIDER

ACTIVE TIME
5 minutes

TOTAL TIME
35 minutes

SERVES
6 to 8

6 cups apple cider

1 apple

1 orange

4 star anise pods

½ teaspoon whole cloves

5 allspice berries

2 cinnamon sticks

I love making mulled apple cider in the fall and winter. It's a great drink to warm up with on a cold or rainy day, and it makes your house smell so good as it simmers. (You could also heat cider in a slow cooker and keep it warm for hours for a party.) I like adding slices of fresh orange to the pot for a bright note that makes the drink even more special.

1. Pour the cider into a Dutch oven or a large pot. Slice the apple and orange horizontally into 4 or 5 rounds and add them to the pot, along with the star anise, cloves, allspice, and cinnamon sticks.

2. Bring the cider to a simmer over high heat, then reduce the heat to low and continue simmering until the flavors have melded, about 30 minutes.

PART FOUR

WINTER

COZY RAINY DAY LUNCH

FOR A RANCHER ON THE CENTRAL COAST, THERE IS NOTHING

better than waking up to the sound of rain. I hear it falling loudly on the porch next to my bedroom and more softly on the roof above me. I get up and walk into the kitchen so I can look out the window and watch it, see it falling on the trees in my yard, the thin curtain making the hills and fields look blurry. The rain isn't heavy, but the sky is dark and it looks like it's going to keep raining all day.

Rain is one of the most important ingredients in ranching, especially in this part of California, where the wet season only lasts three or four months, if we're lucky, and the summers are hot and dry. A year of good rain means abundant grass. It means we can grow our herd and save some money on the hay we'll need to get us through the summer, when we let the grass reseed itself. It means the underground aquifers that our wells draw from will start to refill. Rain is a part of ranching that we have absolutely no control over. We look at the sky, we make predictions, and we hope and pray.

A rainy day on the ranch also means we get a staycation. There isn't a lot of work we can do when it rains. We'll feed the pigs and chickens and let the sheep out, but mostly we'll just stay home and have fun together. The first rainy day also feels unreasonably exciting. The boys wake up and yell, "It's raining!" They learned from an early age that if it's not a school day, they can expect a day of fun at home. Austin pulls on some boots and a jacket and goes into our garden to check the rain gauge. By the end of the day, hopefully we'll get an inch—maybe even more.

The boys and Austin settle in for a day of board games and puzzles. I make everyone some spiced cocoa—a mix of chopped bittersweet chocolate and milk with a hint of cinnamon topped with whipped cream and shaved chocolate that I learned from the señora I lived with when I was studying in Spain—and then pull out some boxes of photos I've been keeping in my office. Having a quiet day gives me an opportunity to start on one of my end-of-year projects: our annual photo album. In the era of digital photos, it can feel old-fashioned to build a physical book full of photos, but for me, printing out pictures is the best way to save memories.

By late morning, however, everyone is beginning to feel antsy. The rain is still going steady, but we decide to take a walk. My kids are obsessed with rain gear. They have whole outfits for the rain: pants that pull on over their rain boots and heavy waterproof jackets to go on top, plus umbrellas. On the other hand, I own almost nothing that's specifically meant for the rain. I'll be soaked through in minutes, but I don't mind the wet at all.

We head up into the hills, along the dirt road, then veer off to follow some small paths the cows have created. We know most of this ranch by heart, but we always hope to find something new on these walks—a place where a fallen tree has opened up a new path or a new view. Today we find an old water tank that must have been left here decades ago, and the boys spot some animal nests and burrows. On our way home, as we walk down the side of a hill, I'm surprised to catch a view of our house, down the canyon, that I don't think I've ever seen before. All the familiar pieces are there—the trees and fields, and the house—but from where I'm standing, it's suddenly fresh and new.

By the time we get back home, it's midafternoon, and I decide to make a hearty lunch that will double as an early dinner. The boys pull off their muddy boots and gear, and I start on a creamy soup of roast squash flavored with fresh sage from our garden. The soup is golden and fragrant, like a little bit of sunshine in our dark day. It's also surprisingly filling, and I know it will keep everyone happy through the evening. While the soup is simmering, I also throw together some grilled cheese sandwiches using a loaf of rustic homemade sourdough that our neighbor Sydni makes fresh every week and a mix of mozzarella, white Cheddar, and Gruyère cheeses. I also spoon some sweet-and-sour onion jam into the filling, to make the sandwiches extra tasty and decadent. For dessert, I'll serve some campfire cookies, a treat I invented to turn s'mores into something I can make ahead and keep around the house.

As we sit down to our meal, the rain is still going strong and the clouds are getting darker by the minute. We feel luckier and luckier with every heavy downpour. We can't predict what this winter's weather will bring—how many wet days we'll get, and whether we'll have enough water in our creeks and wells and fields—but we feel grateful for every minute of today's storm.

SPICED HOT COCOA

ACTIVE TIME
15 minutes

TOTAL TIME
15 minutes

SERVES
4

FOR THE COCOA

2 cups heavy cream

4 ounces semisweet chocolate, plus more for grating

2 cinnamon sticks

¼ cup granulated sugar, plus more to taste

Pinch of cayenne (optional)

2 cups whole milk

FOR THE WHIPPED CREAM

1 cup heavy cream

¼ cup powdered sugar

I fell in love with thick, chocolaty Spanish-style cocoa when I studied in Sevilla. Señora Isabelle, whom I lived with, would make it as a treat to enjoy at any time of day, from breakfast to afternoon to evening. I felt so lucky to be living with her as a student; she acted like a kind of grandmother and cooked many amazing meals. I always think of her when I make this cocoa. The "spice" in this recipe comes from cinnamon, but I've also added the option of a tiny bit of cayenne for anyone who wants a little kick.

MAKE THE COCOA

1. Put the cream in a medium saucepan. Break the chocolate into small pieces and add it and the cinnamon sticks to the pot.

2. Slowly whisk the mixture over medium heat, making sure it doesn't boil, until all the chocolate has melted, about 5 minutes.

3. Add the sugar and the cayenne (if using) and whisk until the sugar dissolves. Add the milk to the pot and bring the mixture back to a simmer. Taste the cocoa and add more sugar if you like.

MAKE THE WHIPPED CREAM

1. Put the cream and powdered sugar into the bowl of a stand mixer fitted with the whisk attachment and whip on medium speed until the cream holds stiff peaks. (Alternatively, whisk the mixture with a hand mixer in a large bowl.)

2. To serve, divide the cocoa among four mugs, top each with a dollop of whipped cream, and grate some chocolate on top.

BUTTERNUT SQUASH
SOUP *with* SAGE

ACTIVE TIME
40 minutes

TOTAL TIME
2 hours

SERVES
6 to 8

Two 3-pound butternut
squash

2 tablespoons unsalted
butter

1 yellow onion, cut into
½-inch dice

½ teaspoon kosher salt,
plus more to taste

1½ quarts Turkey or
Chicken Broth (page 210)
or store-bought

2 tablespoons light brown
sugar

2 sage sprigs, plus
sage leaves for garnish
(optional)

Ground black pepper

¼ cup heavy cream
(optional)

*We grow a lot of different kinds of squash on the ranch, and after the
fall harvest, Katie and I store crates and buckets of them to cook with all
winter long. I like to bring out the squash's natural flavor by roasting it,
then I simmer it with some fresh sage, which grows all year round in my
garden. I also make this soup with other kinds of hard winter squash,
depending on what I have in my pantry.*

1. Preheat the oven to 350°F.

2. Cut the squash in half lengthwise and scoop out the seeds and stringy
membranes. Use the tip of a carving knife to put a couple of long, ½-inch-deep
cuts into the flesh of each of the halves.

3. Put the squash halves in a baking pan, flesh side up, and roast them for
about 90 minutes, until fork-tender. Set the squash aside to cool until it's no
longer too hot to handle.

4. When the squash is almost done, put the butter and onion in a Dutch oven
or heavy-duty pot with ½ teaspoon salt and cook over medium heat, stirring
occasionally, until the onion is beginning to turn translucent, 5 minutes.

5. Scoop the flesh out of the roasted squash halves with a large metal spoon
(without taking the firm layer that forms on the top of the flesh) and add it
to the pot. Add half the stock to the pot. Cook the mixture, breaking up the
pieces of squash with your spoon, on medium heat until hot and steaming, 3 to
5 minutes.

6. Use an immersion blender to puree everything, adding the remaining broth
as you go. (Alternatively, transfer the mixture to a stand blender and process it
until smooth, then pour it back into the pot and add the broth.)

7. Stir in the brown sugar, add the sage, and bring the soup to a simmer.
Reduce the heat to low and let cook, stirring occasionally, until the sage's
flavor has perfumed the soup, about 10 minutes. Taste the soup, adjust the salt
and pepper, and stir in the cream (if using). Remove the sage sprigs before
serving; you can garnish individual bowls with fresh sage leaves, but you
should not eat them.

GRILLED CHEESE *with* SWEET-AND-SOUR ONION JAM

ACTIVE TIME
35 minutes

TOTAL TIME
1 hour, including cooling

SERVES
4, with extra onion jam

FOR THE JAM

3 cups finely diced sweet onion, such as Vidalia or Walla Walla (about 2 large onions)

¼ cup extra virgin olive oil

1 teaspoon kosher salt

¾ cup granulated sugar

1 bay leaf

½ cup balsamic vinegar

FOR THE SANDWICHES

6 ounces low-moisture mozzarella

2 ounces white Cheddar

2 ounces Gruyère

Unsalted butter, at room temperature

Eight ½-inch-thick slices rustic sourdough bread

On a cold night, a grilled cheese sandwich is my go-to meal. Grilled cheese goes with just about everything, and you can make it as simple or as fancy as you want, changing up the type of bread and cheese you use and adding fun ingredients. For this version, I use a mix of cheeses and add some homemade onion jam, which gives the sandwiches an even more complex, sweet-sour flavor—and makes them feel that much more special. This onion jam is also great on sandwiches, burgers, and even steaks. It's easy to pull together, and it keeps in the fridge for a few days.

MAKE THE JAM

1. Combine the onion, olive oil, and salt in a large cast-iron pan. Cook the onion over medium heat, stirring occasionally, until very soft, about 15 minutes, letting them brown a bit on the edges.

2. Use a wooden spoon to spread the onion out evenly in the pan, reduce the heat to low, and sprinkle the sugar on top. Do not stir. Let the onion and sugar cook together, undisturbed, until the sugar dissolves, 2 to 3 minutes. Add the bay leaf and simmer the mixture for 2 minutes, stirring constantly to keep the sugar from burning.

3. Increase the heat to high and add the vinegar (standing back to avoid the steam). Cook, stirring constantly, until the vinegar begins to thicken, about 2 minutes. Let the mixture cool to room temperature, about 20 minutes.

MAKE THE SANDWICHES

1. Cut all three cheeses into large pieces, put them in a food processor, and pulse them together until the texture resembles rice.

2. Generously slather butter onto one side of each slice of bread. Heat a cast iron pan over medium, and place a slice in the pan, butter side down. Top it with one-fourth of the cheese, 1 to 2 tablespoons of the onion jam, and another slice of bread. When the cheese begins to melt, flip the sandwich over. Cook until the cheese is completely melted, another 3 to 7 minutes. Repeat to make three more sandwiches.

CAMPFIRE COOKIES

ACTIVE TIME
20 minutes

TOTAL TIME
*1 hour 40 minutes,
including chilling*

MAKES
12 cookies

1 cup (2 sticks) unsalted
butter, at room
temperature

1 cup packed light brown
sugar

¾ cup granulated sugar

2 large eggs

1 teaspoon pure vanilla
extract

1 sleeve (4.8 ounces)
graham crackers

2 cups all-purpose flour

1 teaspoon baking powder

1 teaspoon kosher salt

4 ounces semisweet
chocolate, roughly
chopped

36 to 60 mini
marshmallows

Maldon salt or other flaky
sea salt

*These treats are basically s'mores in cookie form. I really love s'mores;
we make them on New Year's Eve, and I always have the ingredients
around for parties, so kids can sit around our fire pit and make
them. Eventually, I decided that I wanted a way to enjoy this flavor
combination even without a fire going, so I combined them into huge,
decadent cookies. Now I can bring them to parties or pack them in a
picnic basket. They're perfect all year round.*

1. Line two sheet pans with parchment paper.

2. Put the butter into the bowl of a stand mixer fitted with the paddle
attachment or a large bowl (if using a hand mixer) and beat it on medium
speed until fluffy, about 2 minutes. Add both sugars and beat the mixture until
it's well combined, about 1 minute. Add the eggs and vanilla and beat until
they're just incorporated.

3. Put the graham crackers in a food processor and pulse until they have
a grainy, sandy texture. Transfer 1 cup of the crushed graham crackers to a
medium bowl and mix in the flour, baking powder, and kosher salt.

4. Add half the flour mixture to the butter mixture and beat until combined.
Add the remaining flour and beat again. Scrape the bowl and mix by hand until
everything is fully incorporated. Mix in the chocolate.

5. Roll the dough into 12 equal balls (each about 2 inches in diameter) and
space them out on the prepared sheet pans. Refrigerate the dough on the
pans for at least 1 hour, until fully chilled.

6. Preheat the oven to 350°F.

7. Remove the sheet pans from the refrigerator and bake the cookies for
18 minutes, rotating the pans between the racks halfway through, until they
are golden brown on the edges and just set in the center. Pull the sheet pans
out of the oven. Add 3 to 5 mini marshmallows to each cookie, lightly pressing
them into the cookie's surface. Dust each with a pinch of flaky salt.

8. Bake the cookies for another 2 to 4 minutes, until the marshmallows have
settled into the cookies.

9. Let the cookies cool on the sheet pans for 10 minutes, then transfer them to
a cooling rack to cool completely.

HOLIDAY BAKING PARTY

EVERY YEAR, AT THE START OF THE HOLIDAY SEASON, I MAKE
a bunch of sweet treats and give them to our friends and neighbors—and every year, these same friends drop off their own baskets of homemade goodies for my family to enjoy. This informal exchange is not particular to our area, of course. Farmers, ranchers, and people all over the world have this same tradition. It's a way of sharing what you've grown or made with your community. When I receive a gift of homemade food, I know that someone is giving me their time and care. And they're also giving me something that they themselves love!

This year, to get things started, I've invited Katie and her kids over for a quiet morning baking party—having helping hands makes things go faster and is more fun for everyone. We're planning to make classic sugar cookies that the kids can decorate with icing, molasses lace cookies with white chocolate centers, Mexican wedding cookies with a Central Coast twist, and some fancy-tasting but super-simple espresso meringue cookies. I'm also planning to make some caramel-covered popcorn drizzled with chocolate, some chewy caramels, and of course, our family favorite: the "cowboy brittle" that Austin's mom taught me how to make.

By the time our friends arrive, right after breakfast, I've already preheated the oven (partially to heat my kitchen). I made the dough for the sugar cookies last night, so we start the morning by rolling out that dough and letting the kids cut it into fun shapes. I've been collecting cookie cutters for years, and by now I have a big collection the kids can choose from. I particularly love the classic shapes, like the star, the snowman, and the gingerbread man. My boys usually grab the dinosaur, the cowboy boot, and a cutter shaped like a bone—I don't really get the appeal of the bone, but they love it.

While the kids are busy, Katie and I turn to the sweets that need a bit more care. First we pop the popcorn and make the caramel that we'll mix into it. When it all looks good, we spread it out on a couple of sheet pans to cool; we'll drizzle the chocolate on once the caramel is at room temperature. We also start on the brittle. It has three layers—a crunchier caramel with almonds mixed in and a chocolate layer on each side that also gets a scattering of almonds. Then we make some simple, chewy caramel and pour it into a casserole dish to let it set. Later, I'll cut it into squares and wrap each one in a bit of parchment paper.

When the sugar cookies come out of the oven and the kids have started decorating them, I spoon the batter for the lace cookies onto sheet pans and pop them into the oven. We also start on the more delicate treats, the espresso meringues and the Mexican wedding cookies. The meringues seem sophisticated, but they're actually really easy to make. In fact, I use the same recipe base all throughout the year and just swap out the flavoring. Once the egg whites and sugar are whipped and flavored, the kids help me spoon them onto the sheet pans in irregular dollops.

My wedding cookies are also simple. The base is a classic combination of butter, ground walnuts, and powdered sugar, which gives them their traditional tender and crumbly texture, but I also add minced rosemary and a bunch of orange zest to give them an aroma and flavor specific to this particular part of the world. By the end of the morning, the counters are covered with treats. With the "fun" part done, the kids head down to play in their tree house.

When everything has cooled and set, I pack it up in metal cookie tins that I've ordered just for this purpose. Most people get a mix of everything, but if I know someone really loves one particular kind of sweet, like the brittle, I make them a big package of just that. I nestle small handfuls of each kind of treat into the tin with some parchment paper, then tuck some sprigs of rosemary or pine around them to keep things from rattling around—and to make the boxes feel even more festive. Last, I tie them up with ribbon and mark them with everyone's names.

Tomorrow, my boys and I will jump in the truck and drop them off. Because everyone is busy during the holidays, we usually just pop the tins in mailboxes as a surprise treat. My brother and I used to do this with my mom when we were young, and it's wonderful to do it now with my boys. Many of our neighbors and friends have a signature pickle or jam or baked good that they give out every year. My mom, for instance, is famous for her bread-and-butter pickles, and Katie's mom, Sally, makes delicious chutneys.

For me, these kinds of informal, community-oriented traditions are the best part of the holidays, and I look forward to sharing them with my kids every year. Everything around us—on the ranch and in the world—can change so much from year to year, and the joy of these little traditions, and passing them on, is what gives our holidays their little touch of magic.

CLASSIC SUGAR COOKIES

ACTIVE TIME
35 minutes, plus more for decorating

TOTAL TIME
3 to 4 hours, including chilling and decorating (or longer if you chill the dough overnight)

MAKES
approximately 24 cookies

1 cup (2 sticks) unsalted butter, at room temperature

½ cup granulated sugar

2 large eggs

1 teaspoon pure vanilla extract

2½ cups all-purpose flour, plus more for dusting

½ teaspoon kosher salt

Simple Decorative Icing (recipe follows)

SPECIAL TOOLS

Cookie cutters

Sugar cookies are just about the most classic holiday treats you can make. We do a few batches every year, and the kids have a blast making shapes with their favorite cookie cutters and decorating the baked cookies with colored icing. I divide the icing into lots of small bowls so that we can make as many different colors as we want, and we paint it on with the kind of small paint brushes that usually come with kids' paint sets. Sometimes we're really literal with our designs, and other times we just go wild with the colors; it's a fun and delicious art project to do on a holiday weekend.

1. Put the butter and sugar into the bowl of a stand mixer fitted with the paddle attachment or a large bowl (if using a hand mixer) and beat them together until well combined, about 2 minutes. Add the eggs and vanilla and beat until combined, about 30 seconds.

2. Mix the flour and salt in a medium bowl. Add half of the flour mixture to the butter mixture and beat until just combined, about 30 seconds. Add the remaining flour mixture and beat again until the ingredients are just combined.

3. Divide the dough in half and form each half into a disk. Wrap the disks tightly in plastic wrap and refrigerate them for at least 2 hours or (preferably) overnight.

4. When the dough has chilled, preheat the oven to 350°F. Line two sheet pans with parchment paper.

5. Roll one disk of the dough out on a lightly floured surface to ¼ inch thick. Cut the dough with cookie cutters and transfer the cookies to the prepared sheet pans, leaving 1 inch between them.

6. Bake the cookies for 8 to 10 minutes, until golden and starting to brown slightly along the edges. Transfer them to a cooling rack and let them cool to room temperature, about 15 minutes. Repeat with the second disk of dough.

7. Use colored icing to decorate the cookies as you wish, then set the cookies back on the cooling racks until the icing sets. Store the cookies in an airtight container for 2 to 3 days.

SIMPLE DECORATIVE ICING

2 cups powdered sugar,
plus more as needed

¼ cup whole milk, plus
more as needed

Food coloring

ACTIVE TIME
5 minutes

TOTAL TIME
5 minutes

MAKES
1 cup

1. Whisk the powdered sugar and milk together in a medium bowl until smooth. (If your icing feels too thin, you can add more sugar by the teaspoon; if it feels too thick and won't run at all, add a bit of milk, ½ teaspoon at a time.)

2. Divide the icing among a few small bowls and add food coloring to each (whichever colors you like), 1 drop at a time, mixing after each drop to see how strong the color is.

ESPRESSO MERINGUE COOKIES

ACTIVE TIME
15 minutes

TOTAL TIME
2 hours

MAKES
16 cookies

3 egg whites, at room temperature

2 teaspoons instant espresso powder

¾ cup granulated sugar

Airy meringues might seem fancy, but they're actually one of the simplest cookies around. Just whip egg whites with sugar, add the flavoring of your choice (in this case it's instant espresso powder), and spoon dollops onto a sheet pan. The result is light, chewy, and crunchy all at once. They're so easy, in fact, that I make various kinds of meringue cookies all year, flavored with whatever ingredients I have on hand. These meringues will keep at room temperature in an airtight container for a couple of days.

1. Preheat the oven to 200°F. Line two sheet pans with parchment paper.

2. Put the egg whites into the bowl of a stand mixer fitted with the whisk attachment or a large bowl (if using a hand mixer) and whisk on medium speed until white and frothy and almost beginning to hold soft peaks, about 3 minutes.

3. Keep whisking while slowly adding the espresso powder and then the sugar, little by little. When everything has been combined, whisk the mixture until the meringue holds stiff peaks, about 5 more minutes. Do not overbeat.

4. Use a spoon to make large dollops of meringue on the prepared sheet pans; you should end up with 8 meringues per sheet, evenly spaced. Bake the meringues for 45 minutes, then turn off the heat and let them cool in the oven.

5. When the meringues have cooled, remove them from the pan with a spatula. Store the meringues in an airtight container for 2 to 3 days.

TIP: Don't try to make meringues on a very humid or damp day; the egg whites won't whip up to their full volume.

MEXICAN WEDDING COOKIES
with ORANGE ZEST AND ROSEMARY

ACTIVE TIME
20 minutes

TOTAL TIME
1 hour 10 minutes

MAKES
36 cookies

1 cup raw walnut pieces

1 cup (2 sticks) unsalted butter, softened

1½ cups powdered sugar

¼ teaspoon kosher salt

1 teaspoon pure vanilla extract

½ teaspoon very finely minced rosemary leaves

Zest of 1 orange (grated on a Microplane or zester)

2 cups all-purpose flour

My version of traditional Mexican wedding cookies has a twist: I throw in some very finely chopped rosemary and some fragrant, freshly grated orange zest, which bring a quintessential Central Coast flavor. Make sure to chop the rosemary as finely as possible so that you don't have any large pieces ready to surprise you, and grate the orange on a zester just before adding it to the mix so that you don't lose any of its fragrance (you can even grate it right over the bowl). While I use walnuts for this recipe, because they're grown locally, you can also use pecans.

1. Preheat the oven to 350°F. Line two sheet pans with parchment paper.

2. Put the walnuts in a food processor and pulse until finely chopped.

3. Put the butter, ½ cup of the powdered sugar, the salt, and vanilla in the bowl of a stand mixer fitted with the paddle attachment or a large bowl (if using a hand mixer) and beat until well combined, about 1 minute. Stir in the chopped walnuts, rosemary, and orange zest.

4. Sift the flour into the bowl and mix until you have one big ball of dough.

5. Roll the dough into 1-inch balls and place them on the prepared sheet pans, spacing them about 2 inches apart.

6. Bake the cookies for about 15 minutes, until very lightly brown.

7. Transfer the cookies to cooling racks and let them cool slightly, so they're only warm to the touch, about 5 minutes. Put the remaining 1 cup powdered sugar in a bowl. Gently roll each cookie in the sugar to coat it on all sides, then put it back on the rack. When the cookies have cooled completely, about 30 minutes, roll them in the sugar again to give them a nice white coat. Store the cookies in an airtight container for 2 to 3 days.

MOLASSES LACE COOKIES
with WHITE CHOCOLATE

ACTIVE TIME
35 minutes

TOTAL TIME
2 hours, including cooling

MAKES
12 cookies

½ cup (1 stick) unsalted butter

1½ cups rolled oats

¾ cup granulated sugar

½ cup all-purpose flour, plus more for shaping

¼ cup whole milk

1 tablespoon molasses

1 teaspoon pure vanilla extract

¼ teaspoon kosher salt

1 cup (5½ ounces) white chocolate chips

Delicate, chewy lace cookies are delicious any time of year, but I particularly like making them around the holidays. They're so beautiful, which makes them a great addition to a holiday cookie tin, and the white chocolate gives them a very wintry feel. These are sandwich cookies—the white chocolate goes in between two thin oat-and-molasses wafers and holds them together—so although you'll bake twenty-four cookies, you'll end up with twelve when you're finished.

1. Melt the butter in a large saucepan over low heat, then turn off the heat. Add the oats, sugar, flour, milk, molasses, vanilla, and salt to the saucepan. Turn the heat to medium and cook, stirring constantly, until everything is well mixed and the sugar has dissolved, about 2 minutes. Let the mixture cool to room temperature, about 30 minutes.

2. Preheat the oven to 375°F. Line two sheet pans with aluminum foil.

3. Use two teaspoons to drop teaspoon-size dollops of the cookie dough onto the sheet pans, leaving about 2 inches between each dollop. You'll have 24 cookies. Use the back of a teaspoon dipped in flour to press each cookie down to flatten it slightly.

4. Bake the cookies for 5 to 7 minutes, until bubbly in the center and golden around the edges.

5. Let the cookies cool on the sheet pans for 15 minutes, then carefully peel the foil away from each cookie. (Do not try to peel the cookies off the foil!)

6. Melt the white chocolate in a double boiler (or a large heatproof bowl set over a pot of simmering water) over medium heat, stirring constantly with a rubber spatula, then remove it from the heat.

7. Use a butter knife to cover the bottom of one cookie with a generous layer of white chocolate. Press the bottom of a second cookie onto the chocolate layer to form a sandwich. Set the sandwich cookie on a cooling rack. Repeat with the remaining cookies and chocolate. Let the chocolate in the sandwich cookies come to room temperature and solidify before serving. Store the cookies in an airtight container for up to a week.

CARAMEL CORN DRIZZLED
with CHOCOLATE

ACTIVE TIME
45 minutes

TOTAL TIME
*2 hours 30 minutes,
including cooling*

MAKES
25 cups

¼ cup vegetable oil

1 cup popcorn kernels

1½ cups packed light
brown sugar

1 cup (2 sticks) unsalted
butter

½ cup light corn syrup

1 teaspoon kosher salt

1 teaspoon baking soda

10 ounces dark or
semisweet chocolate chips

SPECIAL TOOLS

Large (10 × 18-inch)
disposable aluminum pan
(optional)

Candy thermometer

Caramel corn is a fun, quick treat to make for a crowd. To get the caramel to really coat all the popcorn (instead of making big clumps), you'll need to heat it in the oven a couple of times as you stir it into the popcorn. To do this, I pour it into a 10 × 18-inch disposable aluminum tray with 3-inch sides; they're easy to find in any supermarket. You can also divide the popcorn between two high-sided sheet pans and reheat it for half the time called for in the recipe.

1. Put the oil and popcorn kernels in a Dutch oven or a very large pot and shake to make sure the kernels are coated. Cover the pot with a tight-fitting lid and set over medium heat.

2. When the popping starts, shake the pot occasionally and turn the pot around on the stove once in a while to avoid having a single hot spot on the bottom.

3. When the popping slows down to just 1 to 2 pops per second, remove the pot from the stove and pour the popcorn into a large disposable aluminum pan, if using, or two sheet pans. You will have about 20 heaping cups. Discard any unpopped kernels.

4. Preheat the oven to 200°F.

5. Combine the brown sugar, butter, corn syrup, and salt in a medium saucepan and heat over medium heat. Melt the butter and sugar, stirring occasionally, then bring the mixture to a rolling boil.

6. Let the mixture boil, stirring constantly, until the temperature reaches 250°F on a candy thermometer, about 5 minutes. Remove from the heat and carefully add the baking soda, standing back in case the mixture creates steam. Quickly stir the baking soda into the mixture until it is thoroughly combined.

7. Quickly pour the caramel over the popcorn (dividing it evenly between the two sheet pans, if necessary) and stir thoroughly to coat the popcorn.

8. Place the caramel popcorn in the oven and bake it for 15 minutes. Remove the popcorn from the oven and stir it well again to coat more of the kernels. Put the popcorn back in the oven for another 15 minutes, then stir again.

continued

9. Remove the popcorn from the pan and spread it out in an even layer on two sheets of wax paper. Let the popcorn cool to room temperature, about 30 minutes.

10. While the popcorn is cooling, melt the chocolate chips in a double boiler (or a large heatproof bowl set over a pot of simmering water) over medium heat, stirring frequently with a rubber spatula.

11. Use a spoon to drizzle the chocolate slowly and evenly over the popcorn in a thin stream, going back and forth across the layer of caramel corn. The chocolate will not totally cover the popcorn, but try to make sure that every piece has at least a little bit of chocolate on it.

12. Let the chocolate cool completely for at least 1 hour, then break up the caramel corn into large pieces to store or serve. Store the popcorn in an airtight container for 2 to 3 days.

HOMEMADE CARAMELS

ACTIVE TIME
25 minutes

TOTAL TIME
1 hour 55 minutes

MAKES
about 115 caramels

½ cup (1 stick) unsalted butter, plus more for greasing

2 cups granulated sugar

2 cups light corn syrup

¼ teaspoon kosher salt

One 14-ounce can sweetened condensed milk

1 cup heavy cream

SPECIAL TOOLS

Candy thermometer

I really love caramel, so I've spent a lot of time perfecting my recipe. The key is to pay attention to the temperature—cook the caramel too long and it will become hard, like a brittle. But if you watch your thermometer while you cook and take the mixture off the heat right away, you can have soft caramels perfect for giving as holiday gifts or using in Fudgy Caramel Brownies (page 29). If you serve the caramel while it's warm, you can also dip apples into it or even pour it over ice cream.

1. Grease a 9 × 13-inch baking dish with butter and line it with parchment paper.

2. Melt the butter in a Dutch oven or large, heavy-duty pot over medium heat. Add the sugar, corn syrup, and salt and cook, stirring continuously, until the sugar has dissolved, about 3 minutes.

3. Add the condensed milk and cream to the pot and place the candy thermometer on the side of the pot so that the bottom is in the liquid but not touching the bottom or side of the pot. Continue to cook the mixture, stirring constantly, until the mixture reaches 240° to 245°F, 15 to 20 minutes, then immediately remove from the heat. If the mixture seems like it might be starting to burn, reduce the heat to medium-low or low and be sure to keep whisking constantly. The caramel mixture will bubble for most of the time and will progressively turn more of a golden-brown color.

4. Pour the caramel into the prepared pan and let it cool to room temperature, at least 1½ hours.

5. Remove the caramel from the pan and cut it into 1-inch pieces. Enjoy right away or wrap each caramel in a square of parchment paper and store in an airtight container for up to 2 weeks.

TIP: To cut caramels easily, put a light coat of vegetable oil on both sides of a sharp knife.

COWBOY BRITTLE

ACTIVE TIME
25 minutes

TOTAL TIME
*1 hour 35 minutes,
including cooling*

MAKES
12 cups

2 cups (4 sticks) salted
butter, plus more for
greasing

2 cups granulated sugar

3 tablespoons water

1 cup sliced almonds

12 ounces milk chocolate
chips

2 cups finely crushed
almonds

SPECIAL TOOLS

Candy thermometer

This sweet, crunchy brittle is a favorite holiday treat among everyone in my family—and is wildly popular with our friends! The recipe comes from Austin's mom, Debbie. She shared it with me years ago, and it introduced me to the technique for making sugar-based candies. This process can seem intimidating, but it's super simple: All you need is a candy thermometer that attaches to the side of the pot and sticks down into the cooking liquid (without touching the bottom of the pot). Then you simply watch the thermometer until the mixture reaches the right temperature, pour it onto a prepared pan, and let it cool. Last, you spread on some melted chocolate and add crushed almonds.

1. Grease two sheet pans with butter.

2. Combine the butter, sugar, and water in a deep pot. Attach a candy thermometer to the side of the pot with the end in the liquid but not touching the bottom of the pot. Cook the mixture over medium heat until it reaches 250°F, about 10 minutes.

3. Add the sliced almonds and stir to combine. Continue to cook the mixture until it reaches 300°F, then immediately pour it onto the prepared pans, dividing it evenly. Do not move the pans around; let the caramel spread naturally. Let the brittle sit until it is just cool enough to safely handle it, about 5 minutes; it should have hardened slightly around the edges and shouldn't be goopy in the center—if it is, wait another minute or two. Gently flip each big piece of brittle over, set it back into the same pan, and use a paper towel to very carefully wipe the butter off the top of the brittle, trying not to break it.

4. While the brittle continues to cool, prepare the chocolate: Melt the chocolate chips in a double boiler (or in a heatproof bowl set over a pot of simmering water) over medium heat, stirring frequently with a rubber spatula.

5. When the chocolate has melted, spread one-fourth of it onto each slab of brittle and sprinkle each with one-fourth of the crushed almonds. Flip both slabs over, placing them back in their pans (it's fine if some of the almonds fall off). Divide the remaining melted chocolate between the two slabs. Spread it out, and sprinkle it with the remaining almonds.

6. Let the chocolate firm up until it has fully hardened, at least 2 hours, then break the brittle into smaller pieces to serve or wrap up. Store it in an airtight container so that it maintains its crisp texture.

NEW YEAR'S EVE

THE MORNING OF NEW YEAR'S EVE IS DARK AND CHILLY.

We had a hard frost overnight, and I can feel the cold creeping in at the windows and under the doors. Outside, the hills are white with a light coating of ice—something we don't see often on the Central Coast. When I exhale, my breath floats into the air; even inside, it's freezing.

Austin brings a huge armful of wood in to get the fires going again, and the house slowly starts to warm up. Then he and the kids bundle up in heavy coats and gloves and head out on a walk to break the ice that is covering the water in troughs in the nearby fields. I put the kettle on the stove, and when it whistles, my friend Jen shuffles into the kitchen. She's visiting from New York, so she's used to cold weather, but she's also used to central heating, so we stand by the fire to stay warm as we drink our tea and make a plan for the day.

Tonight I'll be hosting my family's annual New Year's Eve party. Ever since I was little, my family has invited friends and family to come to the ranch to mark the end of the year. We sometimes go all out for dinner, setting the table with our best china, mixing festive cocktails, and serving special dishes we wouldn't really have at any other time of year. It's a moment to embrace tradition and old-style glamour.

Jen and I start by setting my long dining room table. We use white plates with gold rims that used to belong to my mom's mom and silver that was given to me by my dad's parents. We set out separate salad plates and pressed linen napkins. Along the center of the table, we line up candlesticks with tall beeswax tapers and vases filled with white flowers, then surround them with bunches of greenery from trees around the ranch and big red pomegranates. When we're done, the room feels welcoming and elegant.

ꝑ

I have always loved old things. I grew up watching black-and-white movies starring Cary Grant and Katharine Hepburn, and I always try to take great care of anything my family has passed down to me. I also love old-fashioned dinner parties. When I was little, my job was to set the table. My mom taught me where the salad fork, butter knife, and dessert spoons went at each place. Before dinner, I was also often asked to pass appetizers around, and I learned early on how fun it is to have people over to enjoy a meal.

Throwing this kind of party is an art, and I want my kids to see that taking the time to honor traditions makes holidays feel special. I love ranch life, wearing old jeans and spending every day outside working with animals, but I also love throwing on a dress—maybe even a little lipstick. Embracing both parts of my life makes me feel balanced and brings me joy.

I'm also a big believer in using special, beautiful things. I've never really understood keeping your best belongings safe instead of actually enjoying them. Both my grandmothers used to keep their living rooms pristine and untouched, and while this kept everything in great condition, it also meant these spaces never felt lived in or relaxed. I don't believe that my fancy glasses are there just to be admired. Yes, we keep them on high shelves and don't use them every day, but I don't treat them like they're pieces in a museum. Instead, I get them out for special occasions. Even the kids get to use the fancy stuff; that way, they will have their own memories with it, and it will feel special when I pass these items on to them. A few things have been broken or chipped over the years, but to me, that's far better than never enjoying them.

Once the table is set, I get started on dinner. It's dark early these days, so we've invited people to come over in the late afternoon and enjoy a long, relaxed evening. Like the table, the meal will be special and even a bit old-fashioned. We'll have sautéed chanterelles on toast and roasted marrow bones, baked oysters Rockefeller on the half shell, and some fun cocktails to enjoy them with. The centerpiece of the meal will be a big bone-in rib roast, a fancy, incredibly flavorful cut of meat that I serve only at this kind of special occasion. We'll have it with a creamy horseradish sauce, puffy egg popovers (a classic dish my dad has been making for years), and a colorful, festive salad of greens and bright, seasonal fruit. Some of the dishes take a while to cook but none is actually difficult to make, and I can work on them slowly throughout the day, enjoying the warmth of the kitchen as things roast and bake.

While the meal will be celebratory, it's actually just the first half of the party. In my family, we don't stay up until midnight—we get up way too early for that—so we ring in the new year at nine o'clock by gathering around a big bonfire. It's something we've been doing almost every year of my life, and it's the part everyone looks forward to the most.

I always like to make sure to have the table set and the first bites of food set out when people arrive. This way, even if I'm still in the kitchen putting the last touches on the food—and I usually am—the party can start right away. Just before the guests arrive, I light the candles in the dining room, set up the bar with the ingredients for riffs on classic cocktails, and make trays of the appetizers so people can enjoy them with their drinks. The room fills with the smell of the beeswax candles, and the flames glint off the silver and reflect in the windows.

My parents, our neighbors, and other guests arrive dressed for the occasion in holiday outfits with a bit of sparkle and glamour. We sip our drinks and stand by the fire for a while, catching up on how the holidays have been. I bring the oysters out to the bar, then put the popovers in the oven, so they'll be warm and fresh for the meal. While this party is fancier than most of the get-togethers I throw during the year, it also feels especially cozy with everyone gathered together in the house. The dogs come in from the cold and claim spots on the couch, and the kids take friends to play in their room before dinner. When we eventually sit down to dinner, we swap our cocktails for champagne and toast to the year to come.

After dinner we make some coffee and gather around the fireplace for a big game of charades. Charades is a very serious game in my family. We usually play on both Thanksgiving and New

Year's, and the friends who have been coming to these celebrations for a long time know what to expect and have all learned the rules. We also make sure to get the kids involved with easier and more relatable titles that they'll have fun acting out.

Partway through the game, Austin quickly and quietly slips out and heads down to the flats below our house to get the bonfire started. When it gets close to nine o'clock, everyone puts a warm coat over their party outfit and grabs a hat and scarf, and we all walk down the hill together, drinks in hand, to meet by the fire. It's a clear, cold night, and the million stars feel brighter than ever.

The only other light comes from the bonfire, which is big enough that it casts a warm glow over the whole field. I get out marshmallows, graham crackers, and chocolate bars so everyone can make s'mores. Soon the kids and the dogs are all running around the fire in big, joyous circles, and everyone's fingers are sticky with melted sugar.

As our "midnight" approaches, my mom and I hand out small pieces of paper and pens. It's time for our last end-of-year tradition: setting intentions and getting rid of anything we don't want to bring into the new year. Each person writes down hopes for the new year, or troubles they don't want to bring with them into the future, and then throws each piece into the fire, one by one.

I take a minute to reflect on the challenges we've faced in the past twelve months and think about my hopes and dreams for both my family and the ranch in the coming year. We never know what life will be like from month to month or even day to day—we can't predict how much rain we'll get or how hot the dry season will be. My hope is that whatever happens, we'll keep doing what we've always done: we'll spend our days working with the animals, enjoy our time with family and friends, celebrate our successes, and do our best to change and adapt with the land from season to season. We'll work every day to take care of this place that has nurtured my family and do what we can to leave it even better for future generations.

As I return to the fire, I hear my dad start the countdown: "Five, four, three, two, one . . ."

"Happy New Year!" we all shout in unison, then we hug our friends and family, kiss our kids, and toast to new adventures.

MARROW BONES *with* TOAST

ACTIVE TIME
10 minutes

TOTAL TIME
1 hour

SERVES
8

3 tablespoons extra virgin olive oil

8 marrow bones (about 2½ pounds)

8 garlic cloves, minced

2 teaspoons kosher salt

Ground black pepper

1 teaspoon fresh thyme leaves

1 baguette, cut into eight 1-inch-thick slices

One of the things I've most loved about selling our beef is that it has pushed me to learn how to cook every single cut of meat there is. No part goes to waste. When I started my business, I'd never cooked marrow bones at home, for example, but I quickly discovered that they are really easy to prepare and so decadent. Now I love them! When they're roasted, the interior of the bones—the marrow—becomes soft and tender, and you can scoop it out of the bone and spread it on toast. I ask the butcher who prepares my meat to cut the marrow bones crosswise, so that the bone creates a circle around the marrow, but you can also make this with bones that are cut lengthwise into long troughs.

1. Preheat the oven to 350°F.

2. Spread 1 tablespoon of the olive oil into a large cast-iron pan and set the marrow bones in the pan, cut side up. Evenly top each bone with the garlic, ¼ teaspoon of the salt, a little pepper, and a tiny pinch of thyme leaves.

3. Roast the bones for 45 minutes, covering them with foil for the last 15 minutes, until the marrow is bubbling and has puffed up out of the bones a bit.

4. Spread the remaining 2 tablespoons olive oil in a baking pan and lay the bread on the pan, flipping the slices over once so they get coated with oil on both sides. Toast the bread in the oven for about 10 minutes, until golden brown on the top, then flip the pieces and toast for another 10 mintues on the other side.

5. Serve the bones warm with the bread on the side and a small spoon or knife to scoop the marrow onto the toast.

CHANTERELLES ON TOAST

ACTIVE TIME
15 minutes

TOTAL TIME
25 minutes

SERVES
8

2 tablespoons unsalted butter

2 garlic cloves, minced

1 pound chanterelle mushrooms, cleaned and roughly chopped

1 teaspoon fresh thyme leaves, plus more for garnish

¼ teaspoon kosher salt

2 tablespoons extra virgin olive oil

1 baguette, cut into eight 1-inch-thick slices

Every winter, after the rains have really soaked into the ground and there have been plenty of cold nights, Austin and I head out on long hikes through the hills to hunt for chanterelles. These golden mushrooms are a real treat. Chanterelles are a wild mushroom and can only be found at certain times of year in certain places around the world. Unlike the chanterelles you'll see in markets, the ones we find have often grown to an enormous size, sometimes as big as eight inches across. They're also extremely flavorful. In a good year, we harvest dozens of them. We wash them off with a hose—the idea that you can't use water on mushrooms is a myth—then let them air-dry. When they're ready, I sell them at farmers' markets, but of course we also save some for ourselves. They're wonderful on top of eggs or piled on toast—as I serve them here. If you can't find chanterelles in the market, you can make this dish with your favorite mushroom.

1. Preheat the oven to 350°F.

2. Melt the butter in a large cast-iron pan over medium heat. Add the garlic and cook, stirring, until it is softened but not browned, about 1 minute.

3. Add the chanterelles and stir so that they're evenly coated with the butter. Cook the mushrooms, stirring frequently, until they have lost much of their moisture and have softened, about 8 minutes. (The liquid in the pan should mostly boil away.) Add the thyme and salt and stir everything once to combine, then remove the pan from the heat.

4. While the chanterelles are cooking, spread the olive oil in a baking pan and lay the bread on the pan, flipping the slices over once so they get coated with oil on both sides. Toast the bread in the oven until lightly golden on the top, about 10 minutes, then flip the pieces and toast for another 10 minutes on the other side.

5. Top each piece of bread with a scoop of the chanterelles. Garnish with some thyme leaves and serve warm.

OYSTERS ROCKEFELLER

ACTIVE TIME
30 minutes

TOTAL TIME
1 hour 10 minutes

MAKES
12 oysters

12 oysters

2 tablespoons unsalted butter

4 garlic cloves, minced

4 cups loosely packed baby spinach

1 teaspoon kosher salt

¼ teaspoon crushed red pepper

¼ cup freshly grated Parmesan

¼ cup panko bread crumbs

Flat-leaf parsley, roughly chopped

Lemon wedges

SPECIAL TOOLS

Rock salt

This is a rich dish full of cooked spinach, butter, cheese, and bread crumbs. But the flavor isn't the only reason I make it—it's also easier to prepare than raw oysters on the half shell. Because you're cooking the oysters, you don't have to shuck them. Instead, you can put them in a hot oven until they pop open on their own, which is a lot easier than prying the shells apart! The only extra item you really need is rock salt—a big, coarse type of salt that you can find at most grocery stores—so that you can make a layer to nestle the oysters in, which keeps them steady while they cook.

1. Preheat the oven to 450°F.

2. Wash and clean the oysters well. Set them in a baking pan whole and roast them for 5 to 10 minutes, until they open slightly. Remove them from the oven and let them sit until they are cool enough to handle.

3. Pick up an oyster with an oven mitt (to protect your hand) and use a butter knife to pry it open the rest of the way. Cut the muscles that attach the meat to each side of the shell, then nestle the meat into the deeper, more curved side of the shell and discard the flatter side. Repeat with the remaining oysters.

4. Spread rock salt in a roasting pan or casserole dish to make a layer about ¼ inch thick. Nestle the oyster shells into the rock salt.

5. Melt the butter in a cast-iron pan over medium heat. Add the garlic and cook, stirring, until it softens and some of it turns slightly golden, about 3 minutes. Add the spinach, salt, and red pepper and cook, stirring, until the spinach has just wilted, about 2 minutes. Drain the excess moisture from the spinach, then roughly chop it.

6. Spoon the cooked spinach over the prepared oysters, dividing it evenly among them. Add the Parmesan, then the panko, evenly over the top of each oyster, spreading the panko out to make a nice layer over the shells.

7. Reduce the oven temperature to 350°F.

8. Roast the oysters until the panko is golden brown, about 20 minutes.

9. Garnish the oysters with parsley and serve them hot with the lemon wedges on the side.

GREEN SALAD *with* WINTER FRUIT AND CITRUS DRESSING

ACTIVE TIME
20 minutes

TOTAL TIME
20 minutes

SERVES
8

FOR THE SALAD

4 medium oranges, such as Cara Cara

4 Fuyu persimmons, firm and crunchy

1 pomegranate

¾ pound Manchego

8 cups lightly packed mixed greens

1 cup crushed or chopped Candied Pecans (recipe follows) or store-bought

FOR THE DRESSING

1 medium shallot

2 teaspoons kosher salt

⅛ teaspoon ground black pepper

½ cup freshly squeezed orange juice

½ cup extra virgin olive oil

1 teaspoon Dijon mustard

SPECIAL TOOL

Mortar and pestle

Winter is citrus season on the Central Coast. As soon as the weather gets cold, the farmers' market fills up with all kinds of oranges, lemons, and tangerines. I've always thought it was wonderful how these plants provide exactly what we need at this time of year—bright, sweet flavors to offset dark, cloudy days, plus a hit of vitamin C to help us get through the chilly season. This salad takes full advantage of all the winter fruits we get this time of year: I load it up with orange slices, then add lots of persimmon from the tree in my mom's garden and handfuls of red seeds from the pomegranates we grow below my house.

MAKE THE SALAD

1. Cut the peel off the oranges: First, cut the stem end and bottom off, making sure to remove the peel and the white pith but not too much of the flesh. Set each orange down on a cut end and cut the peel and pith off in strips, going from top to bottom and working your way around the orange.

2. Cut the oranges horizontally into ¼-inch-thick slices and remove any seeds. Cut the persimmons horizontally into ¼-inch-thick slices. Seed the pomegranate. Use a vegetable peeler to shave the Manchego into long strips.

DRESS THE SALAD

1. Thinly slice the shallot crosswise. Put it in the mortar with the salt and pepper and mash it with the pestle to form a rough paste. Put the orange juice, olive oil, mustard, and shallot mixture into a small bowl and whisk together well.

2. Divide the greens among 8 salad plates, then top the greens with fruit slices, pomegranate seeds, Manchego, and pecans. Drizzle the dressing over each salad just before serving.

TIP: I like to seed pomegranates in a big bowl of water, submerging them as I work. The water keeps the juices from staining your clothing, all the white pith floats to the surface, and the red arils sink to the bottom of the bowl.

CANDIED PECANS

½ cup packed light brown sugar

1 teaspoon ground cinnamon

2 tablespoons water

½ teaspoon kosher salt

2 cups pecan halves (8 ounces)

ACTIVE TIME
5 minutes

TOTAL TIME
1 hour, including cooling

MAKES
2 cups

1. Line a sheet pan with parchment paper.

2. Combine the brown sugar, cinnamon, water, and salt in a medium saucepan and heat over medium heat, stirring occasionally, until the sugar has dissolved, about 2 minutes. Add the pecans and mix until the nuts are evenly coated.

3. Transfer the nuts to the prepared sheet pan, spread them out into an even layer, and let them cool and harden completely, about 1 hour, before using or serving.

STANDING RIB ROAST

ACTIVE TIME
25 minutes

TOTAL TIME
3 hours 25 minutes for medium rare, including resting (or longer if it rests overnight)

SERVES
8 to 10

One 7-pound bone-in standing rib roast, at room temperature

10 garlic cloves

5 teaspoons kosher salt

2 teaspoons chopped fresh rosemary leaves

1 teaspoon fennel seeds

1 teaspoon ground black pepper

2 fresh rosemary sprigs

Horseradish Cream (recipe follows)

SPECIAL TOOLS

Kitchen twine

Mortar and pestle

Meat thermometer

A standing roast is my favorite classic holiday-style cut. It's the most well marbled and the most tender, and because it has the rib bones in it, it has a tremendous amount of flavor. Just putting it on the table gives the meal a special quality. This is the kind of thing you might only serve once a year, but it's also particularly good for large family gatherings because it lets you cook high-quality meat for a large number of people.

I always tie up my rib roasts—using the classic method of looping twine around the roast and securing it with half-hitch knots—because when you buy bone-in roasts, most butchers will cut the meat away from the bones so that they're easier to carve and serve. Tying the roast holds the meat against the bones in its original shape, which helps the meat cook evenly and gives it a better flavor. (See my step-by-step photos on the next page for guidance as you follow the recipe. You can always ask your butcher to tie it for you.) I also like to prep and season my roasts the night before I cook them so that they have plenty of time to absorb the flavors of the rub as they sit in the refrigerator.

1. Tie up the rib roast: Set the roast on the counter in front of you with the bones sticking out to one side (your left or right; photo a). Take the end of a long piece of twine and tie it around the roast with a square knot, so the string makes a horizontal line on the part of the meat farthest from you (just inside the first rib bone, about 1 inch from the top edge of the roast). Leave a 12-inch tail on one end of the knot and a much longer piece of twine (ideally still attached to the spool) on the other (b).

2. Make a big loop with the long end of the twine (the piece attached to the spool), twisting the loop once at the bottom, so it crosses over on itself (c). Put that loop over the far end of the meat (sliding the meat through the loop) with the twisted section on top, then tighten the loop around the meat about 1 inch below the first knot; you'll have two loops of string around the meat connected with a small piece of twine running between them (d).

3. Repeat this process until the entire roast is tied up (another 3 to 4 times), making sure the string that connects the loops makes a vertical line down the center of the meat. When you're done, snip the end of the string, leaving a 20-inch tail.

continued

4. Flip the meat over and make sure the horizontal lines of twine are evenly spaced. Take the long piece of string, pull it over the loop closest to it, then push it back under that same loop (so it's looped around the horizontal piece of string). Using that same long piece of twine, repeat this process with each horizontal line of twine, looping it over and then under each piece so that all the horizontal lines are connected by the vertical piece of twine (e).

5. Flip the roast back over and pull the string around the closest horizontal line of twine to secure it. Tie the end of the twine tightly to the other cut end, and then trim both ends so they are only a couple of inches long (f).

6. Put the garlic, 4 teaspoons of the salt, the rosemary, fennel seeds, and pepper into the mortar and mash them together with the pestle to form a rough paste. Rub the paste all over the meat and cover with plastic wrap.

7. Refrigerate the meat for at least 1½ hours to absorb the rub or (preferably) refrigerate it overnight and bring to room temperature before cooking.

8. Preheat the oven to 450°F.

9. Put the roast in a large cast-iron pan, rib side up. Sprinkle on another ½ teaspoon of the salt and roast the meat in the middle of the oven for 30 minutes.

10. Remove the pan from the oven. Flip the roast so that it is bone side down, season it with the remaining ½ teaspoon salt, and top it with the rosemary sprigs.

11. Return the pan to the oven and roast until the meat is 130°F for rare, 140°F for medium-rare, 155°F for medium, or your desired doneness (this takes between 1 and 1½ hours). When you remove the roast from the oven, let it sit at least 20 minutes before carving; the heat in the meat will continue to cook it the last few degrees it needs to reach your desired doneness.

12. Serve with the horseradish cream. (Save the bones for beef stock if desired.)

HORSERADISH CREAM

5 ounces horseradish root, peeled and roughly chopped

3 tablespoons white wine vinegar

2 tablespoons water

1 teaspoon kosher salt

2 cups sour cream

2 tablespoons finely chopped chives

ACTIVE TIME
5 minutes

TOTAL TIME
5 hours or longer, including resting

MAKES
about 3¼ cups

1. Put the horseradish in a food processor and pulse it until it is so finely minced it is almost a paste. You should have about 1¼ cups.

2. Add the vinegar, water, and salt and process everything until it is well mixed.

3. Transfer 1 cup of the horseradish mixture to a medium bowl and add the sour cream and chives. Taste the sauce and add more of the ground horseradish if you like.

4. Pour the sauce into a jar and refrigerate it for least 5 hours or (preferably) overnight to let the flavors meld. Serve in small bowls placed around the table. Store in the refrigerator for 2 to 3 days.

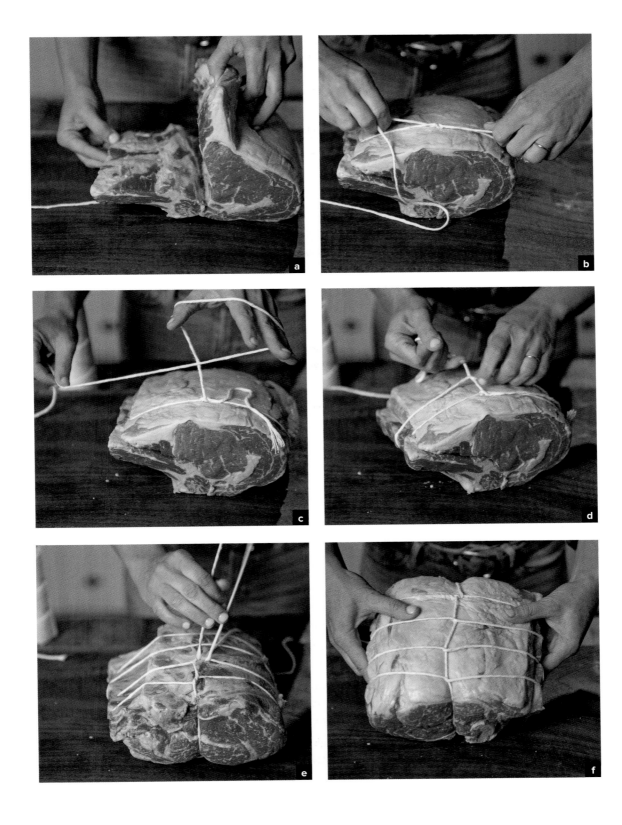

DAD'S POPOVERS

ACTIVE TIME
15 minutes

TOTAL TIME
45 minutes

MAKES
10 to 12 popovers

Unsalted butter, at room temperature, for greasing

2 cups all-purpose flour

1 teaspoon kosher salt

4 large eggs

2 cups whole milk

2 tablespoons vegetable oil

SPECIAL TOOLS

2 popover pans (aluminum)

My dad always makes popovers during the holidays. He originally found the recipe in an old New York Times *cookbook, but he's changed it over the years and made it his own. When I first asked him about his recipe, he told me that the trick is to get the eggs from crazy chickens—a dig at the hens my mom keeps by their house.*

Popovers are basically the same thing as Yorkshire puddings—which are served with meat in the UK—except that for a popover, you don't need meat drippings to season the batter. All you need is flour, eggs, milk, salt, and vegetable oil. You do need a specific pan to make them—it looks like a muffin tin, but the wells are much deeper and there is open space between each well so that heat can circulate. The good news is that the pans are really easy to find, and once you have one, you'll want to make popovers all the time. They're great with eggs for breakfast and go well with flavored butters like my Cranberry Butter (page 216).

1. Preheat the oven to 450°F.

2. Grease the pans generously with butter, making sure there's butter in all parts of the wells.

3. Sift the flour into a large bowl and add the salt. Add the eggs, milk, and oil and whisk until the batter is very smooth.

4. Fill the wells two-thirds to three-quarters of the way full, using up all the batter.

5. Bake the popovers *without opening the oven* for 30 to 40 minutes, until they've risen up a couple of inches above the pans and are light brown on the outside; you want to make sure the outer part of the popovers gets crispy.

6. Remove the popovers from the pans by gently twisting and then lifting them. Serve warm.

GOLDEN STATE OLD-FASHIONED

ACTIVE TIME
2 minutes

TOTAL TIME
2 minutes

MAKES
1 cocktail

Ice cubes

1½ ounces rye whiskey

½ ounce freshly squeezed orange juice

½ ounce Homemade Simple Syrup (recipe follows)

2 dashes Angostura bitters

1 large orange twist

SPECIAL TOOLS

Cocktail shaker with a strainer

An old-fashioned is a perfect holiday drink because it's full of rich, warming flavors. If I make them at home, I squeeze in a bit of fresh orange juice to add the flavor of California winters. When I'm throwing a winter party, I like to make them in batches of a few at a time and set out finished drinks for people to enjoy.

Fill a rocks glass and a cocktail shaker with ice. Add the rye, orange juice, simple syrup, and bitters to the shaker and shake for 30 seconds. Strain the liquid into the rocks glass and garnish the drink with the orange zest.

TIP: The simplest way to make a "twist" with either an orange or a lemon is to use a vegetable peeler; you'll want to get a piece about 2 inches long and 1 inch wide without much of the pith attached.

HOMEMADE SIMPLE SYRUP

1½ cups water

1½ cups granulated sugar

ACTIVE TIME
5 minutes

TOTAL TIME
25 minutes, including cooling

MAKES
2 cups

Combine the water and sugar in a small saucepan and heat them over medium heat, stirring occasionally, until the sugar is fully dissolved. Let the syrup cool to room temperature before using. It can be stored in the refrigerator for up to 1 month.

ACKNOWLEDGMENTS

THIS BOOK HAS BEEN IN THE MAKING AND IN MY DREAMS FOR the last decade, and I could never have done it without the love and support of so many.

I want to thank my husband, Austin, and our boys, Jack and Hank, for being my inspiration to cook every day. Thanks to my parents, who have always been there for me and share my love for connecting people through food, and to Katie Hames, Sarah Perkins, and Blakeney Sanford, whose sisterhood has given me courage while making this book.

Thank you to my Ranch Table team: to Georgia Freedman, for always believing in me, and whose dedication helped me make this book become a reality; to B.J. Golnick, for immediately understanding my vision, and whose stunning photography has brought my dream to life; to Julia Hauben, for creating beauty everywhere she goes; to my wrangler, Standish Hicks Ryan, for being too amazing for words; to Johnny Randano, for always making every day brighter; to my dedicated recipe testers, Kelton Mattingly and Laura Arnold and to my family and friend testers: Candida Canfield, Molly and Greg Heller, Kimberly Berman, Dillon Ryan, Jennifer Sanregret, and Sarah Hunt. I am forever grateful.

A special thank-you to my incredible agent, Alison Fargis, who helped guide me through this exciting process and for believing in me and this project.

To my entire team at HarperCollins/William Morrow: a huge thank-you to my editor, Cassie Jones, whose meticulous eye has been such a gift, and to Jill Zimmerman, Liate Stehlik, Ben Steinberg, Rachel Meyers, Heather Rodino, Renata De Oliveira, Susan Kosko, Anwesha Basu, Sarah Falter, and Kayleigh George.

To my Magnolia family: to Chip and Joanna Gaines, whom I cannot thank enough for giving me the opportunity to share my story—not only on the show, *Ranch to Table*, but also in the pages of this book. I am forever grateful to you both, and "Chip the Bull" will always roam happily on the hills of the San Julian! And to the rest of the Magnolia Publications family, especially Alissa Neely and Kelsie Monsen.

To my family and friends: this book was created over a very long period of time, and I could not have done it without the support of those I love. To my consigliere Sarah Lazin; my brother, Justin Poett; my wonderful in-laws, Debbie and Greg Campbell; mi amiga, Jennifer Drury; my forever adviser, Cáitrín McKiernan; my patient website mentor, Josh Wand; my neighbor Kira Brady; mi hermana, Luz Medina; our dedicated and hardworking Rancho San Julian crew, Billy King, Jenny and Luke Hardin, Angel Hurtado, and Eddie Daltorio; my production team at Conveyor Media; my talented *Ranch to Table* crew; and my extraordinary farmers' market crew.

And, last, to Rancho San Julian, the land that has always been my home, and to all my family who have worked so hard and sacrificed so much so that we all can continue our time here together.

RECIPES BY CATEGORY

DESSERTS AND SWEETS

DRINKS

PANTRY BASICS, BASE RECIPES, SAUCES, AND DRESSINGS

UNIVERSAL CONVERSION CHART

OVEN TEMPERATURE EQUIVALENTS

250°F = 120°C

275°F = 135°C

300°F = 150°C

325°F = 160°C

350°F = 180°C

375°F = 190°C

400°F = 200°C

425°F = 220°C

450°F = 230°C

475°F = 240°C

500°F = 260°C

MEASUREMENT EQUIVALENTS

Measurements should always be level unless directed otherwise.

⅛ teaspoon = 0.5 mL

¼ teaspoon = 1 mL

½ teaspoon = 2 mL

1 teaspoon = 5 mL

1 tablespoon = 3 teaspoons = ½ fluid ounce = 15 mL

2 tablespoons = ⅛ cup = 1 fluid ounce = 30 mL

4 tablespoons = ¼ cup = 2 fluid ounces = 60 mL

5⅓ tablespoons = ⅓ cup = 3 fluid ounces = 80 mL

8 tablespoons = ½ cup = 4 fluid ounces = 120 mL

10⅔ tablespoons = ⅔ cup = 5 fluid ounces = 160 mL

12 tablespoons = ¾ cup = 6 fluid ounces = 180 mL

16 tablespoons = 1 cup = 8 fluid ounces = 240 mL

INDEX

Note: Page references in *italics* indicate photographs.